Mistaken for an Empire

21st Century Essays
David Lazar and Patrick Madden, Series Editors

Mistaken for an Empire

A Memoir in Tongues

Christine Imperial

MAD CREEK BOOKS, AN IMPRINT OF
THE OHIO STATE UNIVERSITY PRESS
COLUMBUS

Copyright © 2023 by The Ohio State University.
All rights reserved.
Mad Creek Books, an imprint of The Ohio State University Press.

Library of Congress Cataloging-in-Publication data available online at https://
    catalog.loc.gov
LCCN: 2022044998
Identifiers: ISBN 978-0-8142-5863-7 (paper); 978-0-8142-8271-7 (ebook)

Cover design by adam bohannon
Text design by Juliet Williams
Type set in Adobe Garamond Pro

♾ The paper used in this publication meets the minimum requirements of the
American National Standard for Information Sciences—Permanence of Paper for
Printed Library Materials. ANSI Z39.48–1992.

Mistaken for an Empire

karga: to carry dusa: suffering; grief puti: white

karga: to carry dusa: suffering; grief puti: white

karga: to carry dusa: suffering; grief puti: white

karga: to carry dusa: suffering; grief puti: white

karga: to carry dusa: suffering; grief puti: white

karga: to carry dusa: suffering; grief puti: white

karga: to carry dusa: suffering; grief puti: white

karga: to carry dusa: suffering; grief puti: white

karga: to carry dusa: suffering; grief puti: white

karga: to carry dusa: suffering; grief puti: white

karga: to carry dusa: suffering; grief puti: white

karga: to carry dusa: suffering; grief puti: white

karga: to carry dusa: suffering; grief puti: white

karga: to carry dusa: suffering; grief puti: white

karga: to carry dusa: suffering; grief puti: white

karga: to carry dusa: suffering; grief puti: white

karga: to carry dusa: suffering; grief puti: white

karga: to carry dusa: suffering; grief puti: white

karga: to carry dusa: suffering; grief puti: white

karga: to carry dusa: suffering; grief puti: white

karga: to carry dusa: suffering; grief puti: white

karga: to carry dusa: suffering; grief puti: white

karga: to carry dusa: suffering; grief puti: white

karga: to carry dusa: suffering; grief puti: white

karga: to carry dusa: suffering; grief puti: white

karga: to carry dusa: suffering; grief puti: white

karga: to carry dusa: suffering; grief puti: white

karga: to carry dusa: suffering; grief puti: white

karga: to carry dusa: suffering; grief puti: white

karga: to carry dusa: suffering; grief puti: white

karga: to carry dusa: suffering; grief puti: white

karga: to carry dusa: suffering; grief puti: white

So I return—

In November 1898, Rudyard Kipling sends a poem to the governor of New York, Theodore Roosevelt. Roosevelt calls it "poor poetry, but strong from the expansionist standpoint."

The title of the poem:

"The White Man's Burden: The United States and the Philippine Islands."

My mother surrenders
her Filipino citizenship at the age of fifteen.

Lola, my paternal grandmother, relinquishes
her Green Card in 1990.

I am born
in Medical City, Mandaluyong, Metro Manila, Philippines,
on November 5, 1994.

I am born a US citizen.

I am assigned Rudyard Kipling's "The White Man's Burden" for my sophomore high school English class in Manila. I am asked to analyze the poem and am too devout to close reading to see anything but irony. What are the elements of the poem? Watch me break them down. Take its sentiment as satire. How could I not?

"Your new-caught, sullen peoples, / Half devil and half child"

Kasalanan mo 'yan.

I learn about the poem's history. Instead of submitting my analysis, I crumple it up until it fits into the pocket of my backpack, filled with balls of failed tests and late reply slips, while my English teacher continues to explain the poem.

Kipling meant every word.

Years later, I type "White Man's Burden" into Google.
Watch me break down—

Kipling means every word.

For a class called "Translated Bodies," I begin a rough translation of the poem into the language of its new-caught, sullen people. I am twenty-four years old. In Los Angeles.

I find myself

beginning again—

Take up the White Man's Burden

karga: to carry
to bear
this burden the flesh
fissures from the weight
of the Lord's mandate
bestowed upon blood

Karga mo ang dusa ng puti

Ten years after living in the United States,

Kipling is the first author writing in English to receive the Nobel Prize in Literature:

in consideration of the power of observation, originality of imagination, virility of ideas and remarkable talent for narration which characterize the creations of this world-famous author.

The Philippines is still a colony of the United States.

                                                    Sorry, not colony.

President Roosevelt writes, "our little brown brothers."

                                                    You're not here.

Macario Sakay, a Filipino who led guerilla warfare against American forces, is sentenced to death.

                                                    Why should you care?

A fragment of a statement he made before he was hanged:

                    "May our independence be born in the future."

May namamatay dito.
                                                    You're not listening.

The first Philippine Assembly. An address by Governor General Howard Taft. A step toward independence. A token of gratitude.
                                                    Translates to

A benevolent experiment remarkable talent for narration.

                                                    remain in place.

An originality of imagination. The incorporation of another state. Simultaneously disavowing

                                    The Philippines remains—

"a virility of ideas."

                        I want to say "lupig," but—Sorry,
                                    not colony either—

The US remains an empire.

                              At ikaw? Nasaan ka dito?

                          Speaking for no one but myself,

Kipling lives.

                          I translate "Take up" to "karga"

In *Translation and Cultural Communication*, Micaela Muñoz-Calvo writes, "Translation plays an undeniable role in the shaping of cultures, of national identities, and it is the vehicle that may make compatible the strengthening of our group identity and consequent knowledge of our own culture with the sharing and learning of other cultures; cultures and their texts becoming accessible and available to international audiences in their own language."

The word *translation* come from the Latin *translat,* meaning "to carry."
Lola instructs me to harden my tongue
as I try to pronounce
"Nakakapagpabagabag"

What differentiates "carry" from "take up"?

Sige, repeat.

This is an exercise in being specific enough to be deemed crucial.

Based on my research, there are no authorized translations of Kipling's "The White Man's Burden" into any Filipino languages, but a Google search offers a number of amateur translations. One comes from thoughtsrandomized.weebly.com. The translation of the author, who cannot be identified aside from an avatar of a person holding a paper bag over her/his/their head, begins with a disclaimer:

"This is an unauthorized translation and should be cross referenced with the original composition." Instead of "dusa," the author decides on "pasanin," which I cannot translate from Tagalog to English without another Google search. The poem begins,

"Kunin ang pasanin ng lahing puti"→"Take up the burden of the white race"

Is it possible to ascertain the aim of the translator through their translation?

May sustansya ba ang sinasalin mo.

                                        Is the burden mine to carry?

Send forth the best ye breed—

Ipadala ang pinakamahusay na sinilang niyo—

The ex-pat laughs

Send: dala: send; what has been sent
the best: pinakamahusay: the most effective
ye breed: na sinilang niyo: ones you birthed

I am unsure

                                        mid-conquest—

Sorry, not conquest. I'm forgetting
The history books say *necessary*

occupation. The history books say *Benevolent Assimilation.* The history books say they saved us from the Spanish. The history books tell us to refer to the Treaty of Paris. The history books say the Philippines was worth $20 million. The history books speak of rebellious Filipinos. The history books say *glory.* The history books are laminated in plastic. The history books say they saved us from the Japanese. The history books gather dust. The history books say they came here to prepare us for sovereignty. The history books are preserved in the digital. The history books say we would not have known what to do

with freedom. The history books make no mention of you. "Which history books?" someone asks.

You need to make a choice—

In the photograph, the barrel of the American soldier's gun points away from the Filipino who gazes upon the foreigner. The barrel of the Filipino's gun is held with both hands. Hawak: to grasp; to possess. Sa akin 'to. What the photograph conveys—two men mid-conversation as if there were no artillery in sight.

"Send forth the best ye breed."
More than ten thousand American soldiers are sent to capture
Manila from the Spanish.

Not capture. I'm sorry—

My father teaches JP, my little brother, how to properly hold a BB gun
and sets up empty cans as targets in the backyard of our house in Metro
Manila. My father never teaches my sisters and me how to shoot a gun.

liberate. The history
books are outdated.
A poem is written to live on.

My father is the son of a retired general. My father is not the reason I
am American.

Ipadala ang pinakamahusay—

Melita Cornel, fourteen years old, boarded a plane at Manila International Airport bound for Los Angeles International Airport. Alone,

She sits by the window in coach. Her first take-off ever. A
breath. Melita glances out the window. Faces forward. Wheels
retract. She shuts her eyes. Let this be over. The upward slant
of the plane. Shift in pressure. The foreign feeling. A pop of
the ear. A breath. A prayer. Her fingernails dig into the skin of
her arm. This will be worth it. She tries. Shift in pressure. To
convince herself. In Pangalatok. The language of the fishing village she was born in. The language spoken in the fishing village
her parents had left her in. Why was she the last of her parents'
children to move to America. Jusko. Why must she be on her
own? A reclined seat. Shift in pressure. Her knees press against
the in-flight safety pamphlet. No space.

Send forth

To complain. Eyes open. Langit. Dagat. Alien heights. Where is she? Able to make out the silhouette of bangkas. How small. Her breathing regulates. Without realizing. Body acclimates. Static velocity. Turns her head. Diyos ko. Nasaan ka? Stares out the window. Transient ripples. To convince herself.

an unauthorized translation of memory—
Unsure if I was ever

The language she knows best. Until. The foreign feeling. Leave them behind. A breath. Nothing to look at. But sky. Acclimating to pressure. Let this be over. "You may unfasten your seatbelts now." A prayer. Why must she be on her own? There is no way back. Diyos ko, kaya ko ba?

told this story. Where am I?

Melita does not sleep. The turbulence refuses to subside.

No way back. Time must pass. Manila International Airport changes its name to Ninoy Aquino International Airport. General Imperial is appointed as the head of Philippine National Police. Time passes. My father and mother employ an architect to construct their dream home. On a former military lot. The second house in what will be a sought-after subdivision. A mile from the airport. My family and I do not flinch at the sound of planes passing above our house.

Where are you?

Melita is now the mother of four children. My mother. At age thirty-six, she flies from Manila to Los Angeles. Unlike the first time she went on this journey, she will not return. Her children don't know that yet. She recites a prayer in English. She sleeps through the turbulence. She remembers—

A quick Google search of the distance between Manila and Los Angeles → 7,305 miles

People also ask:

How many ways to translate "escape"?

To capture the moment mid-conversation between an American soldier and a Filipino soldier in the fields of some unknown province of the Philippines. To send it back to America the image must validate itself with absence. The photographer must present the barren land unoccupied. The photographer must not

> Place them by the margins.
> allow the native to
> litter the scene

let them remain as a mass willing to be seen—The barrel extends beyond the image.

In "Kipling's 'The White Man's Burden' and Its Afterlives," Patrick Brantlinger writes, "Whether or not Kipling's poem had any influence on public opinion, it is unlikely that it affected what the United States government decided to do about the Philippines."

> Permit them to blur.

He writes that "The White Man's Burden" becomes the subject of parody. Most notably, Mark Twain's "To the Person Sitting in Darkness" and Mack Reynolds's *Black Man's Burden*. It is a poem too easy to be ridiculed. Does Kipling care?

By 1902, the Philippine-American war ends

> Mispronunciations litter

with the implementation of the Philippine Organic Act, in which a Philippine Commission would be appointed by the US government as an extension of America's rule over the archipelago.

> the air, starving
> themselves of correction.

Harry Roque Jr., the presidential spokesperson of President Duterte, insists, "We Filipinos are known as a happy, resilient people. We even manage to smile amid difficulties. It is therefore not surprising that we rank high in the global happiness index."

"Bahala na," a phrase used to express one is resigning to what will be, derives from "Bathala na." Bathala: the god usurped by the arrival of Catholicism. Let it be. I turn the other cheek

To carry a burden—

hoping it meets a fist. Lola tells me to kill my enemies with kindness. She tells me I do not have to move to America to succeed—

Bawal tumawid.

A beatitude: "the meek shall inherent the earth."

May namatay dito.

On June 12, 1898, the newly formed government under Emilio Agui-
naldo, the man who will be called the first president of the Philippines,
signs the Declaration of Independence after declaring victory against
the Spanish:

Having as witness to the rectitude of our intentions the Supreme
Judge of the Universe, and under the protection of the Powerful and
Humanitarian Nation, the United States of America

1946: forty-eight years after the Philippine Declaration of Independence
is signed, America grants us full autonomy of our own country. Grant-
ing us independence—

May namatay dito.

Where are you?

I wonder if I am allowed to say *us*. I wonder what belongs to me.
Harvest the dye from carcass.

After replacing my lost passport at the US embassy in Manila, I start receiving security emails. Messages in my inbox after every calamity or threat of terror.

Translates to: Someone is dying here.

Someone dies here.

U.S. Embassy, Manila, Philippines

Emergency Message for U.S. Citizens: Updated Travel Warning for the Philippines

April 22, 2016

THE EMBASSY OF THE UNITED STATES IS TRANSMITTING THE FOLLOWING INFORMATION AS A PUBLIC SERVICE TO U.S. CITIZENS IN THE PHILIPPINES. PLEASE DISSEMINATE THIS MESSAGE TO ALL U.S. CITIZENS IN YOUR ORGANIZATION OR NEIGHBORHOOD. THANK YOU.

The messages don't stop.

EMERGENCY MESSAGE:

This country is not safe.

[DATE]

This country is not safe. This country is not safe. This country is not safe. This country is not safe. This country is not safe. This country is not safe. This country is not safe. This country is not safe. This country is not safe.

This country is not safe. This country is not safe. This country is not safe. This country is not safe. This country

is not safe. This country is not safe. This country is not safe. This country is not safe. This country is not safe. This country is not safe. This country is not safe. This country is not safe. This country is not safe. This country is not safe. This country is not safe. This country is not safe.

This country is not safe

for you. Which one? Ano? You must decide.

Ipadala mo ang anak niyo sa impyerno

Translates to bring: **dala**

> blades between fingers ready
> to grip chattering teeth
> how the second syllable *la*
> demands elongation
> and does not cease
> to be heard

Kipling's poem reads:

"Go send your sons to exile."

I translate "exile" to "**impyerno.**"

← →

"Philippines' President says he'll 'break up' with
the US, tells Obama to 'go to hell.'"
—CNN.com

"Manila less than thrilled at Dan Brown's *Inferno*: City chair-
man lodges protest with author over his description of Philippines' capital as 'the gates of hell' in latest novel."
—*The Guardian*

"Manila as the gates of hell? It's the river Styx too!"
—*Get Real Philippines*

When learning of the legend of the Philippines' national hero Jose Rizal, one cannot forgo his exile by the Spanish government to Dapitan, an island in the Philippines now known as "The Shrine City" for Rizal's affiliation with the rising revolution against the Spanish:

> Rizal, however, does not yearn for revolution. He yearns for reform. Rizal belongs to the Illustrado, the Enlightened Class of educated Filipinos who traveled to Europe to study, to advance their careers, to prove their worth. Jose Rizal, along with other Illustrados, such as Juan Luna, the painter of the Philippines' most prized piece of art, *The Spoliarium,* establishes the publication *La Solidaridad* in 1888. Rizal and the Illustrados prove they are sophisticated enough—

"You're so lucky. I can't wait to leave."

> Rizal returns to Manila in 1892. He continues to push for reform and organizes a group called *La Liga Filipinas.* The Spanish perceive Rizal as a threat to their power. There is no doubting the insurgent language of his novels, *Noli Me Tangere* and *El Filibusterismo.* The end of their rule is imminent.

> That same year, American forces continue to suppress the Garza Revolution in Mexico.

I am asked whether my siblings are jealous I'm in America. When I answer it's their choice to remain in the Philippines, I am met with disbelief. Why would anyone choose the Philippines when they have the privilege of being an American citizen?

> The Spanish arrest Rizal and exile him to Dapitan, south of the Philippine islands, ruled by Muslim datus. His legend grows.

Not in English, of course. Not yet at least.

The revolutionary group, Katipunan, led by Andres Bonifacio, forms in the wake of Rizal's exile.

Why do we use "exile" when we can use "banishment" instead?

> A dirt path paved with concrete.
> Buildings sprout from demolished houses.
> Nandito ka ba?

Rizal escapes Dapitan and soon after is arrested by Spanish authorities.

> I want to be somewhere else.

It's 1896.
Kipling leaves Vermont and returns to England.

Nasaan ka?

A rebellion grows—

> A poem finds its way into a cell.

A dying language is still alive.

sorry, not rebellion—

in the province of Cavite, the Revolution wins their first victory against Spanish forces.

When do we use "force" when we can use "authority?"

In his prison cell, Rizal pens the poem "Mi Ultimo Adios."

On a blood-flood street in Manila, a woman holds the body of her gunned-down husband.

The Revolution continues. Rizal insists he is not a rebel.

A defeat is imminent.
Which one?

I've been back in Los Angeles for a week when I realize my watch is still set to Manila time. How long does jetlag last?

The first International Olympics are being held in Athens, Greece. Out of the fourteen participating nations, the United States is awarded the most gold medals.

Lola asks me about my plans after getting my master's degree. I list PhD programs. All in the States. She shifts and stiffens. "You don't have to be in America to succeed."

Filipino soldiers belonging to the Spanish army are instructed to shoot Rizal. A group of Spanish soldiers stand behind them to guarantee the execution. Rizal's last words, the very same ones spoken by Christ at the Crucifixion:

"It is finished."

Not in English, of course.

I would rather go through tested systems. I don't mind standing in line.

Somewhere
an execution takes place
destined to become legacy—

This is not my memory. It is what I've been told.

You can find it all memorialized online.

A revolution continues.

I want to swear this is true.

In "Veneration without Understanding," Filipino historian Renato Constantino writes that American governor general William Howard Taft chose Rizal as the Philippines' national hero. Unlike Andres Boni-facio and the other members of the Katipunan, the Revolution—

The barrel extends beyond the image. Sorry, not Revolution.

Duterte wins the 2016 election by a landslide. His followers believe that he will impose the sorely needed discipline the country lacks.

Filipino revolutionaries overthrow Spanish authority

The photography of a blood-flood street in Manila.

with the aid of the American army.

"Do not bullshit with me but do your duty, I will die for you. Do your duty and if in the process you kill 1,000 persons because you were doing your duty,

According to the Treaty of Paris, Spain hands over control of the Philippines to the United States for the sum of $20 million.

I will protect you."

I live a mile away from the Manila American Cemetery.

President Trump says Duterte is handling the drug problem the right way.
                    "You speak English so well!"

Juan Luna wins first prize in the *Exposición Nacional de Bellas Artes*. The judges commend him for painting

                    "No! You didn't grow up in Manila!

Luna signs of the Treaty of Paris.

just like the masters—

Imantsa mo ng buhay

Translates to:
"Stain it with life"

A checklist of a Filipino citizen's requirements for obtaining a B-2 (visitor) visa to enter the United States:

- $160.00
- Appointment letter
- DS-160
- One recent photograph 2" × 2"
- Current passport
- All old passports
- Supporting documents

These do not ensure the approval of a visa.

A recommendation on YouTube: *Why Are There So Many Filipino Nurses in the US?*

Because of a friend's father's criminal activity in the US, she is deported back to the Philippines. She continues to apply for entry into the US.

In Eagle Rock, a neighborhood with a large Filipino population in Los Angeles, I spot a billboard written in Tagalog, reminding citizens to report suspicious behavior to the FBI.

I walk into Lola's office and into a conversation between my relatives about *The Assassination of Gianni Versace: American Crime Story.* Lola asks if Andrew Cunanan, the Filipino American serial killer at the center of the TV series, is related to the Cunanans we order ensaymada from during the holidays.

A checkbox: Are you a US citizen?

I enter out from an almost empty room for passport renewal in the US embassy in Manila and stop to observe the long queue extending out the door to apply for a US visa.

Ang swerte ko.

A report from ABS-CBN News: "The latest Department of Homeland Security data shows that in 2016, DHS arrested 263 Filipinos and removed 261 of them."

Niño, my mother's boyfriend, violated the terms of his visa to live in the US. He remains undetected as he works caregiving jobs around El Monte, California. He hopes it stays that way.

When a Filipino wants to travel to the US, they need to prove they will return to the Philippines.

Once again, Lola is denied a visa.

My mother tells me about a family friend who was paid $10,000 to marry a Filipina who wanted to obtain a Green Card.

Ang swerte mo.

My mother has claimed me as a dependent on her tax returns since 2003, the year she left the Philippines and never came back.

I can only write about Mom leaving in present tense:

> The edge of my bed. I am eight years old. Tugging on a black stuffed toy dog. Mom tells me she's leaving for Los Angeles. Last night, I caught my parents sitting on opposite ends of the dining table. They were quiet. At least they weren't fighting again. Flecks of synthetic black fur stick onto my fingernails. She says three months to take care of her grandmother. The door wide open. I can hear my little brother laughing as my sister chases him around the house. Dad isn't home. Mom says she'll be back. She says,

T. S. Eliot, in "Tradition and the Individual Talent" writes, "Poetry is not a turning loose of emotion, but an escape from emotion; it is not the expression of personality but an escape from personality." To be somewhere else: unbound.

> "I don't want anyone to forget me."

A poetry professor suggests I insert more of the "I" in my writing. She suggests I try writing about desire.

> When the first balikbayan box arrives in our house, it is six months after Mom leaves. Clothes too small to fit, almost expired bags of potato chips, unopened boxes of toys, gossip magazines, late birthday cards—She never returns. My siblings

and I visit her in Los Angeles two years later. Camille, a year old when Mom left, confides: "I didn't know that was Mom in the airport. Her hair wasn't short like in the pictures. I was like 'Who are you guys hugging?'"

Whose embrace?

Sino 'to?

Mom didn't leave for greener pastures. There is no color to describe it. There is no noble cause here. I am fifteen years old when I learn it was escape.

I hesitate to say why.

No longer hung in the den
of my father's home:
photographs of nuclear family. The absence:
the arrival of my father's lover.

When I tell my mother
about the missing
photographs, she asks
"How else, anak,
the house has been rearranged?"
She stops me mid-sentence.

"But that mirror,

the crystal mirror yun I had made is still
in the dining room, right? Does she know how
magkano 'yan, how much that costs?"

My mother doesn't care about the photographs.

She asks whether the mirror remains.

Does she know how much that costs?

Lola gave up her Green Card in 1990 to return to Manila. Though she has provided proof that she has no plans of overstaying a visit to the US, she has not been approved for a visa since.

"Nakakaloka. I spent so many years working there, paying taxes. What do they think? I want to stay there?"

Saan ka titira? Saan ka dadamputin?

Despite her grievances, Lola tries again, so she can join my aunt, my cousin, my sister, and me on a trip to New York. The embassy denies her visa.

As a tourist, an American citizen can remain in the Philippines for thirty days without a visa as long as they provide a ticket of departure from the Philippines.

Every month, Lola receives a Social Security check from the US government.

A January 22, 2019, report in the *Philippine Star,* the newspaper I recall scrambling through on Sundays at Lolo's, my paternal grandfather's, house to read the comics section before my cousins got to it first: "The Department of Foreign Affairs has advised Filipinos abroad, especially those in the United States, to follow immigration rules and to avoid overstaying in their host countries."

Why would anyone want to return?

Anong gusto mo?

"This statement comes after the US Department of Homeland Security announced that the Philippines will no longer be eligible for H-2A and H2B visas, which are issued to foreign workers seeking agricultural and non-agricultural work, respectively."

A crossword puzzle clue:
to affirm as true, accurate;
provide evidence.

In 1986 Ronald Reagan signed the Immigration Reform and Control Act, which granted amnesty to illegal immigrants in the United States.

Over empanadas bought from a Red Ribbon, a Filipino bakery chain, in Glendale, Uncle Benjo tells me how he and Dad, after finding out they were eligible for a Green Card, headed to the immigration office as soon as they could. I have not heard this story before. I imagine my father, straight out of graduating from UCLA, walking out of the immigration office ready to secure a future in America. Then I remember a car ride through Fairfax:

> My father tells me, "If it weren't for your Mom. We would have never moved back to the Philippines."

> My parents take my sister Casey and me to a weed-ridden lot in Taguig, Metro Manila. They tell us that this is where our home will be built. Our home will be a house built on military land. I don't know that yet. I think of what color I want my room to be.

> "We could have built a life here."

> The weeds do not know they are weeds.

Uncle Hugh, Uncle Benjo's white partner, interrupts to ask if I know how Lola got her Green Card. Uncle Benjo recoils, "Your lola should be the one to tell you."

Three definitions of confession:

- a formal admission of one's sins with repentance and desire of absolution, especially privately to a priest as a religious duty;

When I try to ask Lola about how she obtained residency in the US she tells me,

- an admission or acknowledgment that one has done something that one is ashamed or embarrassed about;

"You really want me to bring back the past best forgotten? Not a good idea, but I will if you need me to."

- intimate revelations about a person's private life or occupation, especially as presented in a sensationalized form in a book, newspaper, or movie.

Lola should be allowed to forget.

"Masyado kang konsentrado sa nangyari na."

Lola reminds me to stop apologizing.

Under the Immigration and Nationality Act of 1965, my maternal great-grandfather is granted citizenship by the US government for his involvement with the US military in World War II.

I struggle with the tenses.

When Lola narrates stories of her past, she tells me I have permission to write them in a book.

Marie Imperial drives on the freeway for the first time. She's been in Los Angeles for a week. She stays in the right lane until the road narrows. Merge. Brake. Accelerate. A car honks. Too slow. She leaves her left signal on until she finds an opening. Merge. She's been driving since she was twelve years old. Too slow. Honk. She recalls the first time. Out of necessity. Merge. She inhales. Exhales. A prayer. Accelerates. Looking over her shoulder. Signal left. She laughs to herself. Triumphant. Merge. A police car flashing its lights at her. Signal right. She pulls over. He tells her she is driving twenty miles below the speed limit. Her hands still on the wheel. She digs them into—Honk. An accident. The policeman laughs. She tries to laugh. He gives her a warning and tells her to follow his lead when he gets in his car. She follows his driving. Merge. Until the cop car can no longer be seen.

Merge.

This is as true as I can recall.

This is as true as it has been retold.

When Marie becomes a grandmother, becomes Lola, she will not fail to remind me that living in the US isn't the same as being a visitor. She will remind me the greatest gift my mom ever gave me is my American citizenship.

Merge.

1988. Marie returns to the apartment in Los Angeles she shares with my parents (before they are my parents) after spending a month in Manila. Her mother has died. Her father has died. Her first grandchild is about to be born. She sets her luggage down in the bedroom. A pile of mail sits on the dining table. Credit card bills in her name she does not recall applying for. The phone cord cut. The zeros on the bills extend. Thousands of dollars. Her name tainted. She calls each bank. They tell her every form has been signed MCI.

Why do you care?

You weren't there.

My mother is frantic from being found out.

Marie does not want to hear it. I don't know what my father knows. My mother offers her first child as payment. A child not born yet. A child who will ask

"Lola, did you ever feel like you belonged in the States?"

I don't know

if I am five or six years old

when I return to Manila. Return, it doesn't fit. My first memory:

Throttled from sleep onto my image in the mirror. I do not know it yet, but I am in America. A three-bedroom apartment in Folsom, California.

"Where am I?"

The first thought I recall ever having. The mattress undressed. The blinds opened. Crème walls. There's still sunlight. "Where am I?" The evening arrives as a journey through fractures— assembling Lego blocks; an unfinished meal; television commercials; Casey, my then infant and only sister, asleep on the couch. A trip to the grocery store, where I observe everyone else's bodies in their entirety. I spin in circles

to catch myself as third-person, to know—

Return—the word doesn't fit when I recall:

It is the night before we leave for Manila for the very first time. I take the globe from my room and ask Dad where the Philippines is. He places me on his lap and takes my small pointer finger. Together we trace the archipelago

I am supposed to call home.

I hesitate to call home.

I keep two time zones displayed on my phone.

In *Schizophrene,* Bhanu Khapil writes, "Reverse migration is . . . psychotic."

The day we move (back, as I am told) to Manila, a group of women meet us at the airport. It's 1998 or 1999. Lola and Dad's two sisters. My parents push me toward them. I stand firm and run back to Mom, crying.

I don't know who she is.

Lola recalls the day at airport with me over a glass of wine on the balcony of her condominium in Mandaluyong. Her second cigarette burning on the ashtray. A jar of lengua de gata on the table. Through the closed glass doors, the sound of the TV continues.

"That day hurt me so much. Ang close close natin bago ka umalis sa America tapos you didn't want me to hold you."

>Lola teaches me to roll my *r*'s. To strike my *t*'s against the wailing of vowels. For Tagalog is a language of the percussionist born on the edges of breath. A language that mistakes the mouth for hands.

When I call Lola on the phone, I remember—

>I am a child. Lola scratches my back in a 3/4 rhythm. Her smoke-stained voice attempts to sing me to sleep, "Que sera, sera

I stay up until she stops singing and the television comes on.

Whatever will be will be."

My mother is watching the Filipino Channel on her iPad in her bedroom in El Monte, California. She asks me why I'm leaving the room. She asks me why I don't ever sleep in her bed. I do not have to courage to tell her that I am nauseated by her scent.

Kapil continues, "Because it is psychotic not to know where you are in a national space."

I am a child.

My mother prints out the lyrics of *The Star-Spangled Banner* for me to memorize before leaving for ballroom classes. She sings it once for me. I fail to reconstruct its melody.

Roman Jakobson writes, "Such a translation is a reported speech; the translator recodes and transmits a message received from another source. Thus translation involves two equivalent messages in two different codes."

Wala akong maintindihan. Dahan-dahan lang.

Kipling, where are you?

Suddenly, the roads direct me somewhere else and tell me it's been this way for years. Even the GPS knows it. The guard to the gated subdivision I've lived in since I was seven asks me to show ID, to prove this is where my home is.

"Where are you from?"

Para isilbi ang mga kailangan ng bihag

CAPTIVE → BIHAG

To save those in need of capture—
To translate "White Man's Burden"
I cannot rely on myself—I believe

I cannot rely on myself. A new impasse. The same impasse. To reencounter the foreignness of what is supposed to be

a mother tongue.—In the search for equivalences

silence. Fractures speech. A history of deciding

between two languages. Too late.

I write a paper on minimalism as a response to capitalist excess for a class about composition in Filipino. The syntax is wrong. So I write the paper in English. Until two days before the deadline. I have to translate. I tell myself,

I am not translating to honor Kipling's poem. With every word I type from English into Tagalog, I continue to correct myself. I weigh each word like the decision were an objective choice, an inevitability unquestioned. I do not trust my Filipino. I go through tested systems. It's that responsibility.

Captive → Bihag

The syntax is wrong.   The syntax is clinical.

I am asked,

"What language do you think in?"   Ingles-na-ingles! Ayan!

I go through tested systems.

It's never enough.

What are we allowed to forget?

I'm five years old. My father wakes me with a gift, a picture book of Tagalog words to learn.

tatay → father

"Walang silbi" translates to "no use." A common exclamation in Tagalog, spoken during frustration at another's refusal to obey.

I am five years old. I sleep with a laminated purple copy of the *Merriam-Webster* dictionary underneath my pillow. Can words travel through osmosis?

It is important to remember translation is not a science of exactitude. Is remembering enough to not want the signifier to fit?

Who am I to take this on?

silbi → save

Kipling, what responsibility do I have to you? We are from opposing sides. My body cannot be mistaken for an empire. Yet, in your youth, you spoke Hindustani until the servants prompted you to speak in English in the presence of your parents. You wrote of the "palm groves" and "purple fruits" of a country you were born into but couldn't call your own. You returned to India and spoke in a tongue forgotten but embodied. The meaning was no longer there, but the sound settled warm on your English tongue. I, on the other hand—

kailangan → need

During the defense of my paper, my professor tells me

I have nothing to defend.

"Wala akong naintindihan sa papel mo. May estudyante ako galing sa Davao at Cebu at masmagaling sila sa'yo. Paki-explain nalang
yun essay mo. Ba't ang pangit ng Tagalog mo."

Ba't ang pangit → Why so ugly?

He doesn't understand a thing. The syntax is wrong.

Pigil → Halt

Message from Lola, 15:01, 2/27/2019: Read your draft! Some changes
you need not follow!

```
*Kargahin mo *Dalhin mo *Isinilang *Dalhin mo *anak nin-
yong lalaki * Upang pagsilbihan * Upang maghintay * mat-
inding (I dont know paningkaw) *Yuong * Nadamang lungkot
* Buhatin * Pagtiyagaan at pagpasiyensahan mo ng lubos
at pagbibigay *Upang *Upang mahinto ang *Padaliin at
pababawin (Wat is napurol) *Upang makuha ang kinita ng
iba *Upang damputin and kakayanin ng bawat mangga-gawa
*Kargahin mo *Ang pagsisising mas nararapat *binaban-
tayan *Kargahin mo *Tapusin mo ang araw ng kabataan
*Inihahandog *nananakit *ngunit *karunungan *pag-hahato
*kauri *pagsisising *binabantayan *Kargahin *Tapusin mo
*taong *karunungan *kauri
```

Every change, I follow.

At least I try.

In first grade, a boy
(I don't recall
his name)
wrote,
MADAMOT
on the open page
of my math notebook
and I couldn't run
to the teacher
until I knew
what the word meant
but I could taste

a cavalcade
of stop signs
puncturing—

The syntax is wrong.

Para isilbi ang mga kailangan ng bihag
Para isilbi ang mga kinkailangan ng bihag
Para isilbi ang kailangan ng mga bihag
Para masilbihan ang kailangan ng mga bihag

Smoking outside a bar in Bonifacio Global City, Metro Manila, with my cousin, a man comes up to us and says he is from Los Angeles. "Us too! Well, kinda," Chris—my half white cousin—exclaims. Well, kinda—throughout our lives, we've existed in the in-between. When spoken to in English by other Filipinos, Chris makes it a point to respond in Tagalog. Lola frequently remarks, "It's funny how the whitest one is the best at being Filipino."

How does one quantify authenticity?

The stranger talks about how much he hates Manila. He asks me if I can't wait to go back to Los Angeles.

"I missed Manila. It's nice being back here."

He responds, "It's because of the maids, isn't it?"

"It's a lot more than that."

In an article in the *Atlantic,* "My Family's Slave," Filipino American Alex Tizon writes about Eudocia Tomas Pulido, whom he calls his family's slave of fifty-six years.

Manang Lita does not allow my siblings and me to take her out to lunch as a treat for her birthday. She insists she would rather cook for us.

Tizon writes, "When the Spanish arrived, in the 1500s, they enslaved islanders and later brought African and Indian slaves. The Spanish Crown eventually began phasing out slavery at home and in its colonies, but parts of the Philippines were so far-flung that authorities couldn't keep a close eye. Traditions persisted under different guises, even after the U.S. took control of the islands in 1898. Today even the poor can have utusans or katulongs ('helpers') or kasambahays ('domestics'), as long as there are people even poorer.

The pool is deep."

I ask Manang Jean to clean my room before I leave the house. I notice her suppress a smile. My voice is shaking. I'm trying not to slip into English. For a simple sentence, I struggle to find the right words. The syntax is wrong. I'm twenty-five. Manang Jean calls to my sister, "Camille, ang cute nahihirapan si Christine mag-Tagalog." It's cute how hard of a time she's having speaking Tagalog. We laugh and I come home to a clean room.

Tizon calls Eudocia "Lola."

While folding clothes I forget I left in the condo she moved into after Typhoon Ondoy, Lola reminds me that in the States you have to do everything on your own. I am moving to Los Angeles in two weeks.

The first time I do my own laundry, I am a study-abroad student in Liverpool. I am twenty years old. I figure out how to work the washing machine and press the button that begins soaking the load of clothing. I forget to add detergent. I stand in front of the machine until it stops spinning and begin again. I don't know about the compartment where the liquid is placed. I place detergent directly onto the slosh of clothes and start the cycle again.

I smoke a cigarette from the terrace overlooking the backyard. I watch Manang Lita using a pole with a hook attached to it to retrieve my family's laundry on rows of string she strung herself.

"Nakakapagod!"

In my mother's house in El Monte, a cousin asks if I'm fluent in Tagalog. "I've never heard you speak it." Before I answer "Yes," my mom, who hasn't lived in the Philippines since 2003, interjects,

"Only to the yayas."
It's a lot more than that.

yaya → maid

I take the bottle of Corona from the kitchen counter and walk up to my room muttering "Not true. Not true. Not true." I quantify the frequency of my Tagalog. I write in my journal.

anger → galit

In English. I gulp my beer. I take a Xanax. In this house, I find myself passing the time by forcing myself to sleep. I can hear my mother laughing with her relatives. Maybe I am what she thinks I am.

I don't know how to recognize anger—

My mother likes to repeat the story of how she tried to get me to wean from her breast milk:

two years old. Mom dabs hot sauce on her nipple. She screams—

"This is how I knew how intelligent you were."

I grab the towel hung across her shoulder and wipe away the hot sauce. I resume feeding.

"Kalahating-demonyo. Kalahating-sanggol."

"Yaya! Pakidala ng tubig sa kwarto ko." → "Yaya! Can you bring water to my room," is the first sentence I recall speaking in Tagalog without stuttering. Every night before sleeping, I shout it from the top of the staircase.

"Kipling, nasaan ka ngayon? Naririnig mo ba ako? May masasabi ka?"

A friend and I are discussing Alex Tizon's article. She insists,

"The whites don't understand. It's not slavery when you treat them like family!"

I tell my mother how my father's lover M treats the household help and how it's resulted in no one staying for more than a few months. My sister recalls a conversation with her,

"You have to make them sagad kasi you're not just paying them. You're letting them live in your home."

yaya (as verb) → to ask; to implore

My mother loves this. My mother loves when M commits fault. She loves when she can frame herself as morally superior. My mother responds,

"Ay nako, the yayas and drivers loved me kasi! They were like my barkada, and I always gave them 100 pesos."

Lola refuses to enter revolving doors.

When my mom introduces me to new people, she never fails to tell them how I spent most of my life in Manila. She never fails to include, "But she sounds so American," as if this were a compliment, as if there were only one way to sound American, as if everything she says is truth.

My mother's coworker meets me for the first time and exclaims,

"She looks so much like you, Melita."

I am of my father's blood too. I am of my father's blood too. I am of my father's blood too. I am of my father's blood too. I am of my father's blood too. I am of my father's blood too. I am of my father's blood too. I am of my father's blood—

I spit at the mirror when I hear a knock on my door.

Upang humintay sa matinding at mabigat na harness

How to translate "heavy harness?"

      I arrive in my childhood
      home exposed
      sinews of electrical cords hum
      crackling commands   fitting aria
      into dialogue commands obedience
      files down spasmodic tongue
      no longer pronounces

wrung   wrong

My sister's boyfriend was afraid of how much English we speak in our household. Speak, because we continue to do so. Speak. For nothing has changed.

"Nakaka-nosebleed"

"Nosebleed," a term used in jest among Filipinos that refers to one no longer being able to articulate their thoughts in English, usually preceded by a pause then a laugh. A means of saying,

"This is not my language.
My body cannot comprehend it.
It halts me enough to bleed."

Which of my accents gives me away?

M. NourbeSe Philip writes, "Parsing—the exercise of dis-remembering language into fragmentary cells that forget to re-member"
I would rather go through tested systems.

JP, my younger brother, tells me about how the students at his university in Redlands, California, ask him how he can live in the Philippines when it's so violent there.

From the screen of my laptop,
I witness a blood-flood street
in Manila. A woman holds
her dead husband. A pieta.

Can we blame them? The death toll from President Duterte's extrajudicial killings has risen to the tens of thousands.

JP drives on Interstate 5, no faster than everyone else on the road. We're laughing, singing "Hawaiian Roller Coaster Ride" from the *Lilo and Stitch* soundtrack. Red lights flash in the rearview mirror. JP keeps driving. The red lights grow brighter. A siren. "Pull over."

A white police officer walks up to the car and before he can say anything, JP says, "I'm terribly sorry, Sir."

The police officer leans forward. "Do you know how fast you were going?"

He inspects JP's license. Keep quiet. It's from the Philippines. Before JP steps out of the car, I tell him, "Don't forget your passport." I watch through the rearview mirror. The radio plays faintly, "There is nowhere I'd rather be."

Another officer—I assume he is Latino—checks on me. Says to stay in the car. This shouldn't take long. I'm afraid to look back. I watch the cars driving past me, trying to estimate their speed. JP returns, holding a ticket.

In 2017 President Duterte receives a phone call from President Trump: "I just want to congratulate you because I am hearing of the unbelievable job on the drug problem."

I tell JP, "I've never heard you say, 'I'm terribly sorry.' It's so polite."

JP responds, "It was something Jon Snow said in *Game of Thrones*."

In *Puro Arte: Filipino on the Stages of Empire,* Lucy Mae Burns writes, "The Filipino man's access to whiteness and American social practices is mediated by his desire to learn, mimic, and ultimately perform."

JP tells me the Latino officer told his white companion to let him off the hook. He tells me the white officer insisted on bringing him to the precinct.

Something easy, something specific enough to make questioning awkward. Around a white audience, I can say whatever I want.

                                                                    In the dream,
I can be believed.
                                        I run from dirt field to dirt field
                                                    from being asked why
                                          I speak English so well to—

My siblings and I rank each other on who is most Filipino. We play a drinking game where we can only speak in Tagalog for the duration of an hour; each time one of us slips into English we take a shot of tequila.

"Christine will be the first to give up."
                                        "Nakaka-nosebleed, 'di ba?"

JP and I drive to our uncles' house. It's been six months since JP moved to California. He tells me that he's starting to like living here. He says his accent is changing.

They're right.

                                                        "Sumuko ka!"

I tap out before I get too drunk.

I write a poem with the refrain "indio child"; I hear an ex-lover:

"Why do you always talk about being brown in your writing?"

Who am I accountable for?

The blueprint of a tongue is a crossfire

aftermath syllable dance   this stranger
on lookout   for the tropic strike
invader sound   I sand
down the grave-
               l croak

of my mother's   consonants
          she too disguises   in white

silence   the "'di ba" with full stop
   a period marks   translation
"right"   /   "you know" this stranger
is a threat   of questions

beckons for the brown   to give more than practice-
   d one lines   when do I decide

nothing   escapes history
   this stranger is a hand-me-down hyphen mirror
holds the cleaver   to my throat
   'til the vocal cords bleed

something beyond   local color

Sa ibabaw ng wagayway at mabangis—

Translates to wayward: **wagayway**

> a word so precise
> the mouth
> sways in the space
> of its utterance

yours is a history of being subdued
yours is a history of being subdued
yours is a history of being subdued
yours is a history of being subdued
yours is a history of being subdued
yours is a history of being subdued
yours is a history of being subdued
yours is a history of being subdued
yours is a history of being subdued
yours is a history of being subdued
yours is a history of being subdued
yours is a history of being subdued
yours is a history of being subdued
yours is a history of being subdued
yours is a history of being subdued
yours is a history of being subdued
yours is a history of being subdued
yours is a history of being subdued
yours is a history of being subdued
yours is a history of being subdued

Yung bago mong nadamang lungkot

Your new, despondent capture.

In a photo taken inside the Igorrote Village at Luna Park in Coney Island in 1905, a white man dressed as Uncle Sam is photographed with an Igorrote family—a mother, father, and their two children.

Taken from their villages,

the Igorot people of the Cordillera region of the Philippines are brought to Coney Island to show the savagery of the Filipino nation to American audiences. An artificial village is built to stage native authenticity for the ecstatic eyes of white audiences,

> to justify the colonial project taking place in the Philippines. Build your nipa huts. Make yourselves at home. Denude until body. For everyone to see.

Uncle Sam looks like an emaciated Beetlejuice. But no one calls his name. A scowl. No one asks him to intervene. Take up the White Man's Burden. Whose voice am I taking on? Tear the shirt on your back and wrap it around your waist. Only native garb. He looks down at the Filipino woman, sliding his long, gangly arms onto her shoulder, believing his touch is a blessing she has yet to deserve.

And the woman—what is she thinking?

I want to say "pigil" but use "resist" instead.

I must learn how to breathe.

In *Camera Lucida,* Roland Barthes writes, "Once I feel myself observed by the lens, everything changes: I constitute myself in the process of 'posing,' I instantaneously make another body for myself, I transform myself in advance into an image."

Translates to "It feels like the white audience is staring at me."

Translates to "We Filipinos are known as a happy, resilient people."

In 1992 performance artists Coco Fusco and Guillermo Gomez-Peña devised *Two Undiscovered Amerindians,* a piece based on the practice of bringing indigenous peoples of Asia, Africa, and the Americas to the United States and Europe to be exhibited. In her essay, "The Other History of Intercultural Performance," Fusco notes, "The exhibits also gave credence to white supremacist worldviews by representing nonwhite people and cultures being in need of discipline, civilization, and industry." Fusco and Gomez-Peña called themselves "representatives of Guatinau," a fictional people located in the Gulf of Mexico. Intended as satire, the performance showcased Fusco and Gomez-Peña living in a golden cage where they performed traditional tribal tasks and took photos with audience members for a dollar. Fusco writes, "As we assumed the stereotypical role of the domesticated savage, many audience members felt entitled to assume the role of the colonizer, only to find themselves uncomfortable with the implications of the game."

A woman from Arkansas comes up to me and asks "Do the people in the Philippines all carry switchblades? I have a friend who's Filipino and he and his dad practice all the time." I tell her we don't.

She insists I'm lying.

Fusco and Gomez-Peña worried that their piece might have been too heavy handed, too obvious to a crowd they assumed was already familiar with the ethical implications.

"We Filipinos are a happy, resilient people."
Bawal tumawid.

I tick "American" on the box that asks for nationality. It's more convenient that way. There are days I feel like an impostor. There are days where I strangle my throat with the flag of my country—

"Which one?"

Fusco notes that one woman argued she and Gomez-Peña were too white to be indigenous people.

"Why do you always talk about being brown in your writing?"

To justify the conquest of the Philippines,

Not conquest.

                                        I was taught we weren't ready.
Where am I?

                                                Where are you?

I am learning to be less grateful.

When faced with the dilemma/the reality of Christianized Tagalogs in Manila whose almost Western demeanor threatened the Americans' occupation of the Philippines, Dean Worcester turned to the indigenous tribes of the Philippines and instructed them to remove any articles of clothing that would signify "a civilized people." Never photographing them mid-action, Worcester placed his subject standing at the center of his ideal backdrops: the jungle and a white wall.

A friend is accused of appropriating indigenous culture at the Silliman Writers Workshop for setting her story in Banaue, a mountain province eight hours away from Manila—the region we call home. In her room in an affluent subdivision in Metro Manila, we argue against the accusation. We're better than that. We talk about

Imperial Manila
From Wikipedia, the free encyclopedia
Imperial Manila is a pejorative epithet used by sectors of Philippine society and non-Manileños to express the idea that all the affairs of the Philippines, whether in politics, economy and business or culture, are decided by what goes on in the capital region, Metro Manila, without considering the needs of the rest of the country, largely because of centralized government and urbanite snobbery. Empirical research finds that Imperial Manila and its persistence over time has led to prolonged underdevelopment in Philippine provinces.

what we are limited to write.

How can I be certain that the language of Kipling's "new-caught sullen people" was Tagalog? How can I be certain of the necessity of translation?

The specimen on display. In one photograph, Worcester employs his own body as marker. Side-by-side with a tribe member of the Igorot people. The contrast of light accentuates the contrast of skin. But they do not stand against the white wall. Instead, the jungle. Worcester, concealed in starched uniform under the heat of the tropic sun, asserts that he is not a specimen. While Worcester stands erect like a schoolboy posing for a class photo, the Igorot man sets all his weight on his right hip. Flamboyant, uncaring. This specimen barely reaching his shoulder. This specimen—

One reason Duterte was elected was the promise of displacing Manila as the center of the Philippines.

the image to send back—

Barthes called the target of the photograph the *spectum* rooted in *spectacle*: to be maimed by the eye. The *studium*: what compels us to look at the photograph, that which catches our attention. How small, this Filipino. How animal.

a return—

"You're too paranoid. You think everyone is out to get you."

Ninang, my mestiza aunt, hands me a bottle of glutathione pills that will lighten the color of my skin. I am twelve years old. I see ads for these pills on billboards scattered along Manila's skyline. I take the pills every day for a month. When I stop, Ninang asks if I've run out of my supply. Years later, a nurse will visit the family office once a week and inject glutathione into Ninang's arm. I ask her why she does it.

"You can always be whiter."

Lying down on our bed, Payton begins to laugh. She entwines her fingers into mine and brings our hands into the light. "We're like yin and yang."

In *Eros the Bittersweet,* Anne Carson writes, "Paradox is what takes place in the sensitized place of the poem, a negative image from which positive pictures can be created."

At 5'5", I'm five inches shorter than Payton. I don't want to keep looking up at her.

In "If," Kipling writes,

There is so much to forget.

"If you can dream—and not make dreams your master.

Payton messages me to stop dwelling on what happened between us.

"When it's over, it's over. You're just hurting

If you can think—and not make thoughts your aim."

when you realize things and then come to me with those realizations."

Kargahin → Carry

Kalahating-demonyo, kalahating-sanggol

Translates to half-devil, half-child
I have no trouble translating this line.

"Christine, kain na. Lalamig yun pagkain mo."

I read a news report about a Filipino Canadian boy who sat in the cafeteria of his school in Quebec. Like I do every time I eat a meal in Manila, the boy simultaneously used a spoon and fork to eat his lunch, instead of just a fork. A teacher caught him and called it "dirty and disgusting."

A YouTube recommendation: a video of a white man using his hands to eat lechon in a village in the Philippines.

I do not know how to turn on a stove until I am twenty-three.

I imagine there was rice on the boy's plate. I imagine how he put the spoon in his right hand and the fork in his left hand, how he used the spoon to scoop the rice from his plate while the fork guided the "ulam" into the spoon's path, how he stabbed the piece of meat with his fork and cut it with the curved edges of his spoon, how he used the spoon to pick up every last morsel of rice on the plate. When I was younger, Lola used to tell me I would pick up each piece of leftover rice on my plate in purgatory.

When the Spanish arrived in the Philippines, they saw Filipinos eating with their hands, gathering food with their fingers. The thumb sliding across the palm to deliver rice mixed with ulam into their mouths. The Spanish wrote about it in their books. Aghast at the way we ate. We needed to be saved—
　　　　　　I need to stop saying "we." I wasn't there.

I sit across from my mother at the dining table and ask her why she eats with her hands. "It's easier for me. I grew up eating like this." My younger siblings pick up the habit. I don't. At home, they raise one leg on their chair while the other hangs above the floor as they gather their food with their right hand and use the left to take large gulps of water.

I tried a few times, but each time, rice slipped out of my hand and onto the floor just before reaching my mouth.

"Sinayang mo ang pagkain."

"Sinasayang mo ang trabaho ng iba."

The dirty kitchen—there's one in my grandfather's house too: the house we lived in after we moved from Folsom, a house we still call home—is where the everyday meals are cooked. I remember when Mom would cook steaks in the "special" indoor kitchen once a month for dinner. She would let the cuts of steak marinate in a mixture of salt, pepper, and lemon in a large casserole dish. When my mom would leave the kitchen, I would watch the yaya—I forget her name—mash potatoes on the kitchen island, and grab a spoon to join her. I felt useful. When I go over to friends' houses, I notice they have "dirty kitchens" too. The dirty kitchen is reserved for the yayas.

What sounds better, *the yaya* or *yaya?*

Lola says not to call the yayas by their first names alone. It's disrespectful, unless you're an adult. I'm somewhere between five and six years old. There were never yayas in Folsom. It was just Dad, Mom, Casey, and me.

"Make sure you say 'please' and 'thank you' whenever you ask them to do something. You can also say 'Ate' instead of 'yaya.'"

Ate, meaning older sister. *Ate,* used to show respect to women who are older than you.

"But you told Casey to call me 'Ate,'" I tell my Lola, trying to get out of being called anything other than Christine by my younger sister.

"It doesn't mean the same thing when Casey calls you 'Ate.'"

I stick to "yaya" unless the maid is much older, in which case, I use "Manang."

When a maid is a Manang, even her employers refer to her as such. A Manang demands more respect. A Manang is the covert head of the household. In Ilocano, a Filipino language spoken in the Ilocos region 251 miles away north of Manila, Manang means "older sister." From the Spanish "hermana."

"Kain na!"

The first night in Manila after moving from Folsom. The first dinner in Manila. A table full of food. Unknown to me. Sour tamarind soup I learn is sinigang. Blood pork stew I learn is dinuguan. Pinakbet. Kare-kare. What is familiar? Rice. I eat it with nothing. Until Lola places a sliced mango on my plate and instructs me to eat it with rice. "You'll like it." I see my cousins doing the same. Morsels of rice swirl with the saccharine mush of mango.

I spit it out.

"Walang utang na loob!"

I go to bed hungry.

I go to a bed I share with my parents in the spare room of my grandparents' home. I go to bed wanting to be in my own bed: my bed in Folsom.

In first grade, a classmate passes me a questionnaire to fill out. One of the questions: "What is your least favorite food?" I write down "Filipino."

Twenty years later, in an Airbnb in Madrid, a friend and I will lie down drunk on a queen-sized bed and list all the Filipino food we miss.

We fall asleep, craving—

Upang itago ang banta ng sindak

To conceal the blade—

President William McKinley, December 21, 1898:

Finally, it should be the earnest wish and paramount aim of the military administration to win the confidence, respect, and affection of the inhabitants of the Philippines by assuring them in every possible way that full measure of individual rights and liberties which is the heritage of free peoples, and by proving to them that the mission of the United States is one of benevolent assimilation substituting the mild sway of justice and right for arbitrary rule.

In an article titled "From Indio to Filipino" in the *Philippine Star,* Elfren S. Cruz writes, "In searching for this Filipino, it is important to look back at history and remember that before the 1880s, the term 'Filipino' actually referred to the people of Spanish parentage born in the Philippines. The Malayan, native born inhabitants of the Philippine islands were called 'indio' or 'indigenta.' This class or group occupied the lowest level in a highly stratified class society."

This is corroborated by multiple documents and taxonomies of inhabitants and natives of the islands of the Philippines during the era of Spanish colonization. One such document is Jean Mallat's *The Philippines: History, Geography, and Customs* from 1846:

The Indio is attached to the master who knows how to correct him properly and makes him feel the master's superiority without treating him disdainfully. Crimes against persons are very rare in Manila and still rarer in the provinces; murders are hardly heard of.

I'm forgetting what I've learned:

to correct the flatness
pinch the nose
of the indio child
to pleat holes
wide enough
to inhale
the sea
through clogged
pores of city

how much of nature is malleable
how much does it take to strangle
the urge to sing

**HEAD-HUNTING, DOG-EATING, WILD
PEOPLE FROM PHILIPPINE ISLANDS**

HEAD-HUNTING. DOG-EATING. WILD PEO-
PLE FROM PHILIPPINE ISLANDS.
Illustrating tribal life. manners. customs. cos-
tumes and industries. during a limited engage-
ment at

CENTRAL PARK
Market and Eighth
THREE GOLD MEDALS AT PORTLAND EX-
POSITION.

Opens Saturday, November 4th

unlatch the indio child
its mouth
from the ashen teat of its mother
tongue to wean
onto a new language

THE FILIPINO COULD EXCHANGE THE WAR
CLUB FOR THE BASEBALL BAT READILY

He could exchange the war club for the baseball bat readily.

until it no longer tastes

foreign until it refuses

grinding consonants
when we sand down
its teeth

THE FILIPINO'S OLD HABIT OF RUNNING AMUCK
WILL AID GREATLY ON THE FOOTBALL FIELD

on an asphalt suburban street
the indio child   plays bato bato pick   correct to rock
paper scissors piko   correct to hopscotch
the indio child always quick to answer

                                                                            yes.

If you want *intense whitening,* look closer.

If you want
intense whitening,
look closer.

chair corrects the squat
fork corrects the hands
shoes correct the gait
labor corrects the indolence
speech corrects the silence

once discovered   no longer—the indio

child always quick to answer   "Yes

                                    yes, i am a mistake
                         oo, kalahating-demonyo
                                    yes, i am a mistake
                         oo, kalahating-demonyo
                                    yes, i am a mistake
                         oo, kalahating-demonyo
                                    yes, i am a mistake
                         oo, kalahating-demonyo
                                    yes, i am a mistake
                         oo, kalahating-demonyo
                                    yes, i am a mistake
                         oo, kalahating-demonyo
                                    yes, i am a mistake
                         oo, kalahating-demonyo
                                    yes, i am a mistake
                         oo, kalahating-demonyo
                                    yes, i am a mistake
                         oo, kalahating-demonyo
                                    yes, i am a mistake
                         oo, kalahating-demonyo
                                    yes, i am a mistake
                         oo, kalahating-demonyo
                                    yes, i am a mistake
                         oo, kalahating-demonyo
                                    yes, i am a mistake
                         oo, kalahating-demonyo
                                    yes, i am a mistake
                         oo, kalahating-demonyo
                                    yes, i am a mistake
                         oo, kalahating-demonyo
                                    yes, i am a mistake
                         oo, kalahating-demonyo
                                    yes, i am a mistake
                         oo, kalahating-demonyo
                                    yes, i am a mistake

advertisements say I am"

on the screen, the priest commands
"remove the veil"

                                  a sleeping infant
to be baptized   no longer concealed

      Unfair 'di ba?
      'Wag magalit mag-Gluta**MAX**!
      Your *fair* advantage.

the priest   does not mask

THE FILIPINO'S FIRST BATH
McKinley—"Oh, you dirty boy!"

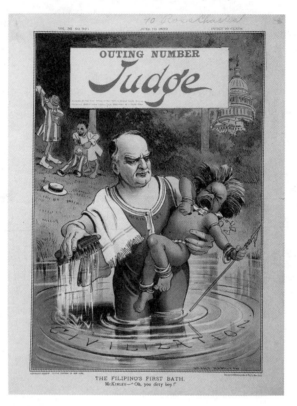

THE FILIPINO'S FIRST BATH.
McKinley—"Oh, you dirty boy!"

the horror   the brown reveal
on the screen   an antidote

BIOLINK SOAP
naturally whitens skin

NATURALLY WHITENS SKIN

BIOLINK

(Lola tells me her teacher would)

press the child's knees
onto a litter box
of mung beans
when its fingers
slip from rosary

HIS WATER BUFFALOS OUGHT TO GO WELL IN TANDEM

indio child answer

"yes, i am a mistake. tell me

SPEAKING FROM EXPERIENCE. (Through Professor Marconi's wireless telegraphy) AMERICAN INDIAN (To Filipino—*Be good, or you will be dead!*

"SPEAKING FROM EXPERIENCE. (Through Professor Marconi's wireless telegraphy)"
"AMERICAN INDIAN (to Filipino) -- 'Be Good, or you will be dead!'"
Judge, Arkell Publishing Company, New York; circa 1899 [artist: Victor Gillam]

what i am."   indio child,

cement specimen into archive—

FROM WAR DANCE TO CAKE WALK IS BUT A STEP!

FILIPINO EXPANSION.

From the war dance to the cake walk is but a step.

Padaliin ang salita

Private William Grayson's account published in *Freedom,* February 6, 1899:

"In a moment, something rose up slowly in front of us. It was a Filipino. I yelled 'Halt!' and made it pretty loud, for I was accustomed to challenging the officer of the guard in approved military style. I challenged him with another loud 'Halt!'

[The Filipino] shouted Halto!   to me."

Inuulit para maintindihan

Halt! Halt! Halt! Halt! Halt! Halt! Halt! Halt! Halt! Halt! Halt! Halt!

Halto! Halto! Halto! Halto! Halto! Halto! Halto! Halto! Halto! Halto!

Halt! Halt! Halt! Halt! Halt! Halt! Halt! Halt! Halt! Halt! Halt! Halt!
Halt! Halt! Halt! Halt! Halt! Halt! Halt! Halt! Halt! Halt! Halt! Halt!
Halt! Halt! Halt! Halt! Halt! Halt! Halt! Halt! Halt! Halt! Halt! Halt!
Halt! Halt! Halt! Halt! Halt! Halt! Halt! Halt! Halt! Halt! Halt! Halt!

Halto! Halto! Halto! Halto! Halto! Halto! Halto! Halto! Halto! Halto!
Halto! Halto! Halto! Halto! Halto! Halto! Halto! Halto! Halto! Halto!

Halt! Halt! Halt! Halt! Halt! Halt! Halt! Halt! Halt! Halt! Halt! Halt!
Halt! Halt! Halt! Halt! Halt! Halt! Halt! Halt! Halt! Halt! Halt! Halt!
Halt! Halt! Halt! Halt! Halt! Halt! Halt! Halt! Halt! Halt! Halt! Halt!
Halt! Halt! Halt! Halt! Halt! Halt! Halt! Halt! Halt! Halt! Halt! Halt!
Halt! Halt! Halt! Halt! Halt! Halt! Halt! Halt! Halt! Halt! Halt! Halt!
Halt! Halt! Halt! Halt! Halt! Halt! Halt! Halt! Halt! Halt! Halt! Halt!
Halt! Halt! Halt! Halt! Halt! Halt! Halt! Halt! Halt! Halt! Halt! Halt!
Halt! Halt! Halt! Halt! Halt! Halt! Halt! Halt! Halt! Halt! Halt! Halt!
Halt! Halt! Halt! Halt! Halt! Halt! Halt! Halt! Halt! Halt! Halt! Halt!

Halto! Halto! Halto! Halto! Halto! Halto! Halto! Halto! Halto! Halto!
Halto! Halto! Halto! Halto! Halto! Halto! Halto! Halto! Halto! Halto!
Halto! Halto! Halto! Halto! Halto! Halto! Halto! Halto! Halto! Halto!
Halto! Halto! Halto! Halto! Halto! Halto! Halto! Halto! Halto! Halto!
Halto! Halto! Halto! Halto! Halto! Halto! Halto! Halto! Halto! Halto!
Halto! Halto! Halto! Halto! Halto! Halto! Halto! Halto! Halto! Halto!
Halto! Halto! Halto! Halto! Halto! Halto! Halto! Halto! Halto! Halto!
Halto! Halto! Halto! Halto! Halto! Halto! Halto! Halto! Halto! Halto!
Halto! Halto! Halto! Halto! Halto! Halto! Halto! Halto! Halto! Halto!
Halto! Halto! Halto! Halto! Halto! Halto! Halto! Halto! Halto! Halto!

Halto! Halto! Halto! Halto! Halto! Halto! Halto! Halto! Halto! Halto!
Halto! Halto! Halto! Halto! Halto! Halto! Halto! Halto! Halto! Halto!
Halto! Halto! Halto! Halto! Halto! Halto! Halto! Halto! Halto! Halto!
Halto! Halto! Halto! Halto! Halto! Halto! Halto! Halto! Halto! Halto!
Halto! Halto! Halto! Halto! Halto! Halto! Halto! Halto! Halto! Halto!
Halto! Halto! Halto! Halto! Halto! Halto! Halto! Halto! Halto! Halto!
Halto! Halto! Halto! Halto! Halto! Halto! Halto! Halto! Halto! Halto!
Halto! Halto! Halto! Halto! Halto! Halto! Halto! Halto! Halto! Halto!
Halto! Halto! Halto! Halto! Halto! Halto! Halto! Halto! Halto! Halto!
Halto! Halto! Halto! Halto! Halto! Halto! Halto! Halto! Halto! Halto!
Halto! Halto! Halto! Halto! Halto! Halto! Halto! Halto! Halto! Halto!
Halto! Halto! Halto! Halto! Halto! Halto! Halto! Halto! Halto! Halto!
Halto! Halto! Halto! Halto! Halto! Halto! Halto! Halto! Halto! Halto!
Halto! Halto! Halto! Halto! Halto! Halto! Halto! Halto! Halto! Halto!
Halto! Halto! Halto! Halto! Halto! Halto! Halto! Halto! Halto! Halto!
Halto! Halto! Halto! Halto! Halto! Halto! Halto! Halto! Halto! Halto!
Halto! Halto! Halto! Halto! Halto! Halto! Halto! Halto! Halto! Halto!
Halto! Halto! Halto! Halto! Halto! Halto! Halto! Halto! Halto! Halto!
Halto! Halto! Halto! Halto! Halto! Halto! Halto! Halto! Halto! Halto!
Halto! Halto! Halto! Halto! Halto! Halto! Halto! Halto! Halto! Halto!
Halto! Halto! Halto! Halto! Halto! Halto! Halto! Halto! Halto! Halto!
Halto! Halto! Halto! Halto! Halto! Halto! Halto! Halto! Halto! Halto!
Halto! Halto! Halto! Halto! Halto! Halto! Halto! Halto! Halto! Halto!
Halto! Halto! Halto! Halto! Halto! Halto! Halto! Halto! Halto! Halto!
Halto! Halto! Halto! Halto! Halto! Halto! Halto! Halto! Halto! Halto!
Halto! Halto! Halto! Halto! Halto! Halto! Halto! Halto! Halto! Halto!
Halto! Halto! Halto! Halto! Halto! Halto! Halto! Halto! Halto! Halto!
Halto! Halto! Halto! Halto! Halto! Halto! Halto! Halto! Halto! Halto!
Halto! Halto! Halto! Halto! Halto! Halto! Halto! Halto! Halto! Halto!
Halto! Halto! Halto! Halto! Halto! Halto! Halto! Halto! Halto! Halto!
Halto! Halto! Halto! Halto! Halto! Halto! Halto! Halto! Halto! Halto!

Halt—

"Well, I thought the best thing to do was to shoot him. He dropped. If I didn't kill him, I guess he died of fright."

I am six years old. Lola is scratching my back to put me to sleep when she tells me I need to start speaking

in Tagalog.

"Why?"

"You're Filipino. You were born here."

I write down "American" as my nationality.

It's more efficient that way.

I am still translating "White Man's Burden"—

Sinasalin ko ang dusa ng puti

Where do you call home?
Where do you call home?
Where do you call home?
Where do you call home?
Where do you call home?
Where do you call home?
Where do you call home?
Where do you call home?
Where do you call home?
Where do you call home?
Where do you call home?
Where do you call home?
Where do you call home?
Where do you call home?
Where do you call home?
Where do you call home?
Where do you call home?
Where do you call home?
Where do you call home?
Where do you call home?
Where do you call home?
Where do you call home?
Where do you call home?
Where do you call home?
Where do you call home?
Where do you call home?
Where do you call home?
Where do you call home?
Where do you call home?
Where do you call home?
Where do you call home?
Where do you call home?

I live in California I live in Manila I live in between I live with my family I live away I live with my father I live alone I live with my mother I live with my grandmother I live trying to make sense of where I live I live where bullfrogs hum I live across from stray cats I live beside the unoccupied house of a disgraced politician I live near peacocks I live near a river I live within walls I live within windows I live locking doors I live in an apartment I live without paying rent I live worrying about the day I'm going to have to pay rent I live in the Philippines I live in the United States I live with my passport on me at all times I live on speculation I live on evidence I live in the home my mother left I live where I want to belong I live on a road left unpaved I live on invitation I live exiled I live between time zones I live searching I live in the Philippines I live in the United States I live with my dog I live because of war I live seven thousand miles away from my dog I live against a screen I live dodging phone calls I live without voicemail I live far from home I live in an immigrant home I live in a native home I live in a hybrid home I live in tradition I live under construction I live keeping silent I live in someone's screams I live where I wasn't born I live where no one can find me I live here I live in the past I live in aporia I live in the Philippines I live in the United States I live where it floods I live without ancestors I live in close quarters I live with my father I live with trespassers I live too far from the center I live without a center I live where I can destroy continuously I live in avoidance I live repairing I live where I can succeed I live where I was born I live where my parents were born I live where my grandmother cannot return I live with my siblings I live with my brother I live alone I live by church bells I live with restraint by monuments I live where stones were thrown at the window of my family's van I live being served I live being denied I live beyond my means I live in exposure I live in the Philippines I live in the United States I live through protection I live in the city I live in the valley I live on an island I live through discovery I live without thinking I live in an old colony I live in a new colony I live where the stranger tells me I live where everyone wants to be I live somewhere dangerous I live where I used to run away I live in a hundred year old home I live beside a field of weeds I live in a new development I live where everyone feels safe

Where do you call home?
Where do you call home?
Where do you call home?
Where do you call home?
Where do you call home?
Where do you call home?
Where do you call home?
Where do you call home?
Where do you call home?
Where do you call home?
Where do you call home?
Where do you call home?
Where do you call home?
Where do you call home?
Where do you call home?
Where do you call home?
Where do you call home?
Where do you call home?
Where do you call home?
Where do you call home?
Where do you call home?
Where do you call home?
Where do you call home?
Where do you call home?
Where do you call home?
Where do you call home?
Where do you call home?
Where do you call home?
Where do you call home?
Where do you call home?
Where do you call home?
Where do you call home?
Where do you call home?

I live where no one feels safe I live under guidelines I live in a house painted white once yellow once peach I live without coordinates I live where Google Maps tells me I live I live under surveillance I live without boundaries I live near the equator I live between mountain ranges I live where I don't want to be I live in question I live like there is an answer I live in a state I live in a boundary I live in airplanes I live where there are earthquakes I live in the Philippines I live in the United States I live away from my mother I live with my mother on the weekends I live in the home my mother ran away from I live in a room once lilac now gray I live ruled over by a dictator I live in what they say is a liberated country I live toward progress I live as a model citizen I live as exception I live without question I live where I grew up I live where I say I grew up I live where I didn't grow up I live waking up to sirens I live somewhere distant I live where there is water I live where there is drought I live on abundance I live in the Philippines I live in the United States I live where my family says I live I live where the documents say I live I live as evidence I live without a visa I live on fault lines I live where it makes me sick I live where I can breathe I live in a trapped nation I live in a sanctuary I live in a liberated nation I live on soil I live on wood I live in an artificial city I live paying rent I live in fear of a sudden passing I live in the Philippines I live in the United States I live not knowing where I live I live where the stray dogs piss on road I live in comfort I live without knowing my neighbors' names I live in the familiar I live with strangers I live on bonds I live on disputed land I live on inheritance I live on a title I live without security I live under guidelines I live where doors are locked I live inside concrete I live where I don't go hungry I live noticed I live where there used to be a field I live where my mother killed a pet snake I live where Lola sleeps I live passing time I live for no one I live selflessly I live wanting I live waiting for a place to live I live in the house I watched my parents live in I live in an immigrant nation I live in the West I live a day late I live in the Philippines I live in the United States I live through verification I live where no one hears me I live refusing to speak I live between two cities I live in between I live where you live I live in a renovated house I live where it used to be empty I live inside the question: Where do you call home

Ang gaspang ng hangin dito.

Mounds of rubble gather into pavement. Bottles of Red Horse beer, cigarette stubs, decaying sampaguita flowers. People walk past an abandoned building. I walk past an abandoned building. No one stops. Buildings keep popping up. Spiderwebs of yellow scaffolding buried in black net. "May namatay na dito."

Ang ganda dito parang sa pelikula, parang wala kang problema. Nakakasilaw yun araw nila. Hindi ako pumapawis. Nauuhay lang. Hindi ito yun boses mo. Pwede tayong tumira dito.

The walls covered with posters. The posters torn. It will all be torn down soon. Photoshopped white models lounge on airbrushed beaches. The billboards keep popping up. There's always a broken shoe on the road. "It's always summer here."

SLOW

MAY NAMATAY DITO

Alam niya kung saan ka tatakbo.
May alam sila sa'yo. Alam nila na hindi ka galing dito.
Alam nila may tinatago ka. Alam nila nahihiya ka. Nakikita
nila sa kayummanggi. Naririnig nila sa tigas ng salita.

The expat laughs. Protection:

Natatawa yun mga taga-rito. Ikaw, 'di ba? Taga-rito ka, 'di
ba? Naririnig nila na taga-rito ka. Nalilito sila pag-sinasabi mo
hindi ka dito isinilang. Nalilito nanaman sila. Nalilito ka. Saan
ka sinilang?

a gated community. Guards take turns keeping out the unknown. After shifts, they unbutton their uniforms and ride their motorbikes away from villages with civilized names—Forbes, McKinley Hill, Corinthian Hills, the list goes on. They find solace

Pasimple ka. Wala kang naranas. Burgis na burgis. Ano yun nirananas mo? Ano ba ang gusto mo? Ah! Hindi mo alam. "Hey, what's up? Are you headed to LA over the weekend?" Wow naman. Kano.

in returning to the unknown. Outside a university coffee shop, a young girl, no older than my seventeen-year-old sister, sells cigarettes to stressed-out college students without IDs. I ask the driver what's causing traffic. We pass the corpse of a woman in a daster by a motorbike. Policemen gather. The young girl selling cigarettes tucks 20-peso bills in between her fingers. She knows which brands are the most popular. She keeps stacks of them underneath the plastic stool with three legs. "Gusto niyo po ng menthol?" Later in the day, I buy a pack from her before I go into the coffee shop to tell my friends about my day.

Ang gaspang ng hangin dito. Tumatawa nalang ako.

An ambulance stalls in traffic. I hear the ex-pat laugh. He knows I don't belong.

Alam niya kung saan ka galing. Teka, saan ka ba babalik?

Tigilin ang mga inaasahan mo

Lola cries over the phone.
"What have I accomplished?"
I am 7,929 miles away from her.
"All I've done is grow old."
The poem is not in order.

Upang kuhanin ang kaya ng bawat manggagawa

I write it out on paper. I know something's not right. I tell my instructor this is the first time my writing feels like it has stakes. *Stakes in what?*

Upang nakawin ang ginawa ng manggagawa.

To stake one's claim to something. How much of this is mine?

Upang dakipan/magnakaw ang trabaho ng manggagawa.

A retranslation: To take the work of workers.
                    To steal someone else's work.

Upang damputin ang trabaho ng mangagawa.

None of it feels right. I turn the words over so much I coat them in a bitter lacquer. What do I ingest?

Upang tumanga ang ginawa ng iba.
Kalahating-demonyo, kalahating sanggol.
Upang humili ng pinagtrabaho ng iba.

My mentor from undergrad and I meet up in a pinball bar in Queens. She reads a recent poem of mine. "The blueprint of a tongue is a cross-fire . . ." She tells me it's good. She notices I'm incorporating Tagalog. She asks me how I feel about the influx of Filipino American poets writing about their identity. I answer it's great. A pause. She's waiting for me to say more.

I answer, I'm afraid of giving in to trends.

In *Immigrant Acts,* Lisa Lowe writes, "Such reductions contribute to the aestheticizing commodification of Asian American *cultural* differences, while denying the immigrant histories of material exclusion and differentiation . . ."

I'm afraid of anything I do

"Why do you write so much about being brown?"

feeling inauthentic—

The syntax is wrong.
I am asked if I've ever written a poem in Tagalog. Why should I? Ang
pangit ng Tagalog ko.

It's 2015. In my mentor's office in Ateneo de Manila University,
a university founded by Jesuits priests in 1859, my mentor reads
a poem of mine and asks me why I italicize Tagalog.

Why must the language be oblique in the face of English? I do it because
that's how I've seen it done. I imitate what I read

'til the vocal cords bleed

something other than local color.

Kargahin mo ang dusa ng puti

You're My Foreignoy/Foreignay is a competition on the popular Filipino noontime variety show *Eat Bulaga!* In the Philippines, noontime variety shows are at most four-hour-long spectacles in which every second must be filled with frenzy and pandemonium. Foreigners, non-Filipinos, compete to prove to the audience that they are "Filipino at heart." They wear traditional Filipino clothing, perform songs in Tagalog, and attempt to answer questions in the native tongue. The crowd erupts. The hosts emphasize that the contestants are "100 percent foreigners." One contestant from England claims, "The Philippines feels like home."

No one really talks about the episode where the British Empire colonizes Manila.

Amílcar Cabral writes that it is not the Westerners we should hate but the system that allows them to sustain power.

WE'RE ABOUT TO HAVE EVEN MORE FUN!

Are we all ready?! Everyone can be part of **#itsmorefuninthephilippines**

All the amazing photos, even the words used for the new Philippine tourism campaign were sourced from real travelers' posts - with permissions of course, and the DOT's deepest thanks. So jump in too!

We can't wait to see YOUR posts in the **# itsmorefuninthephilippines** stream.

Queen of Versailles began as a documentary studying wealth through the building of David and Jackie Siegel's own version of Versailles in Florida, but then transformed, once the 2008 recession hit, into a documentary chronicling both the loss and the maintenance of the Siegels' wealth. I notice all their nannies are Filipino. Once they speak, there is no mistaking it.

One of the Filipino nannies in an interview says, "Since I was young, I've been dreaming how I wish I could go to America. Every Filipino, it's our dream to have our own house. Those Filipinos that was here, they have their families in the Philippines, and they have big houses. I bought a piece of land, so if God permit I can go home, maybe I will build a house for that piece of land that I bought. I need some money to go home. If you go without money, it's not easy. So I need to save some money."

Nostalgia means a longing to return to one's home, a pathological homesickness. Where do we call home? We surrender to memory. We retreat. Until time returns us to our present setting, forcing us to forget. The pain that arises not from the inability to return to a specific space, but escape into an irretrievable time.

Where do you call home?

Filipinos are known for their effusive hospitality. Instead of "Welcome to our home," visitors are greeted with "Welcome home. Here is the best we have to offer. Here is a meal that will bond us for eternity."

Merge.

When Ferdinand Magellan and his crew landed on the shores of Homonhon in 1521, Rajah Humabon, the leader of the local tribe, did not resist baptism.

THE PHILIPPINES WELCOMES YOU AGAIN
The Philippines is excited and ready to warmly welcome visitors from foreign nations!

The buildings continue to pop up.

Jean Mallat writes, "We have already noted that the Indio is very skillful and a good imitator."

Alden Bula—in regard to foreigners messing up the pronunciation of Tagalog words on *You're My Foreignoy*—writes, "It's a funny way for us Filipinos at getting our own revenge. I guess laughing at their errors is our way of getting back at them and dealing with our insecurity and their race superiority. . . . Its success is also due to colonial mentality, a bias toward the West. For us, Pinoys, we are ecstatic to see Amboys and other Caucasians . . . speak our language, sway to our music, and step on our dances."

Merge.

My mother watches only TFC: The Filipino Channel. She asks me to drive so she can watch *Ang Probinsyano* on her phone. My mother giggles. She won't stop. I dig into the gas pedal. I scratch my face. I swerve. She won't stop. I want to hear anything but her laughter.

Hospitality: The Core of a Filipino Soul

The Filipino nanny in *Queen of Versailles* continues, "The [Siegel] children are really attached to me. I really love them like my own, since I do not have my family here. It's just that the last time I see my kids, my youngest one, he's only seven years old, and now he's twenty-six. The Siegel kids, they always say, 'Nanny, I love you,' one thing that I never heard from my children. So I'm happy for that. I miss them."

Where is the line between servitude and hospitality?

In 2007, video circulated on YouTube of an American named Travis Kraft cooking chicken adobo while reciting the recipe in Tagalog. When my dad shows it to the family, they laugh and mock his accent. How he butchers the language while remaining faithful to it the whole video. I laugh too, then my sister reacts, "Christine, he speaks Tagalog like you!" And we all laugh. More than a decade later, I look through the rest of his videos and find out Travis is an ex-pat residing in the Philippines. I recall an article in the *Guardian* I stumbled upon years ago with the headline,

"Why are white people expats when the rest of us are immigrants?"

Lola tells me how much she loves Jochem, the Dutch foreign exchange student residing in my grandparents' home; how he speaks English, how his accent carries a sophistication to it. As his stay extends, he begins to incorporate Tagalog into his own vocabulary. Ending his sentences with "na," "diba," and "palang." Lola calls him her ninth grandchild. The night before he leaves, he gathers the family in the living room and holds a makeshift award show where he awards each member of the family a superlative. He never returns. That's okay. We don't visit him either.

The first time Akira, the Japanese foreign exchange student, has a meal in my grandparents' home, my grandfather asks if Akira knows anything about how the Japanese treated Filipinos during World War II. The rest of my family, including myself, sit in silence until Lola diverts the conversation. Lola never calls Akira her ninth grandchild. He leaves. We don't notice.

"10 Things We Love about a Filipino Home"
—*Real Living* magazine

When two American tourists call Filipino food "disgusting," it causes an uproar online.

Merge.

In an episode of TLC's *90 Day Fiancé*, Larry, a manager at a McDonald's in the US, refuses to eat a suckling pig his fiancé "Jenny" and her family prepared for him. This suckling pig is called "lechon." Especially for poor families in the Philippines, since the lechon costs more than what the family can afford, it is served during the most special of occasions. To refuse it is to refuse sacrifice.

Where is the line between hospitality and servitude?

Filipinos are a happy and resilient people.

On October 18, 2003, President George W. Bush addresses the Philippine Congress:

"America is proud of its part in the great story of the Filipino people . . ."

Halt! Halt! Halt! Halt! Halt! Halt! Halt! Halt! Halt! Halt! Halt! Halt!
Halt! Halt! Halt! Halt! Halt! Halt! Halt! Halt! Halt! Halt! Halt! Halt!
Halt! Halt! Halt! Halt! Halt! Halt! Halt! Halt! Halt! Halt! Halt! Halt!
Halt! Halt! Halt! Halt! Halt! Halt! Halt! Halt! Halt! Halt! Halt! Halt!

". . . Together our soldiers liberated the Philippines from colonial rule. Together we rescued the islands from invasion and occupation."

Halt! Halt! Halt! Halt! Halt! Halt! Halt! Halt! Halt! Halt! Halt! Halt!
Halt! Halt! Halt! Halt! Halt! Halt! Halt! Halt! Halt! Halt! Halt! Halt!
Halt! Halt! Halt! Halt! Halt! Halt! Halt! Halt! Halt! Halt! Halt! Halt!
Halt! Halt! Halt! Halt! Halt! Halt! Halt! Halt! Halt! Halt! Halt! Halt!

His speech is met with roaring applause.

Hindi kasya.

This speech is given two months after Mom leaves for Los Angeles.

I'm trying to make a connection here.

It doesn't fit, does it?

On October 20, 1944, General Douglas MacArthur returns to the Philippines two years after he remarks

"I shall return."

The phrase remains in the Filipino psyche as a promise of certainty, of salvation.

Lola tells me of her father hiding in the mud from Japanese soldiers. She pulls out a photograph of her father, who will lead the whole of the Philippine army, walking alongside MacArthur.

Lola asks me why I look so rattled.

11,736km
Distance from Los Angeles to Manila

I've been back in Manila for four days. "The drive here was stressful," I say. On the way to the family office, I hit a traffic cone by the hazard zone of a freeway and drove away from a police officer gesturing to me to pull over. I kept going. I didn't stop.

Lola responds, "Ay, have Willy drive for you. That's why he's here. That's what we're paying him for.

Kawawa ka naman."   "Poor you. You need to rest."

Ang alamat ng walang kasarian bagay

The legend of objects with no identity.
I need to start packing up my things.
I need to figure out what to leave behind.
"Make sure you have your passport!"

At anihin ang kanyang gantimpala

I type "American Propaganda Poster in the Philippines 1889-1940" on Google Image Search. A result:

A poster promoting American expansion with the headline "The Administration's Promises Have Been Kept." Portraits of William McKinley and Theodore Roosevelt are at the center of the poster; behind them, images proving the improvements and progress made—from Democratic to Republican, from a run on the bank to a run to the bank, from Spanish rule in Cuba to American rule in Cuba. Below their portraits, the poster reads "THE AMERICAN FLAG HAS NOT BEEN PLANTED ON FOREIGN SOIL TO ACQUIRE MORE TERRITORY BUT FOR HUMANITY'S SAKE."

In *American Tropics: Articulating Filipino America,* Allan Punzalan Isaac writes, "The mimetic mandate creates symbolic infractions on two fronts. First, Filipinos as colonial subjects were being forced to mimic a fantastical projection of the American subject. They must accede to the signs of America—in speech, clothes, mannerism, and cultural consumption.

For a school pageant,
I have no choice
in the fabric
my mother
dresses my body in:

white rayon gown
silver sash pinned

across: ***Miss America.***

Second, mimesis, as with all desire, falters."

In *Decolonising the Mind,* Kenyan writer Ngugi Wa Thiongo writes of the privileged status of English in once-colonized nations such as Kenya, "English became the measure of intelligence and ability in the arts, the sciences, and all the other branches of learning. English became *the* main determinant of a child's progress up the ladder of formal education."

"Have you written a poem in straight Tagalog?"

My mother tells me she does not understand my poems. "Nakakanosebleed. Ang galing ng anak ko! Your English is too deep, anak, for Mommy to understand."

"Kaya mo ba?"

In my elementary school, I was known as the girl who could not speak in Tagalog. During Filipino class, any of my attempts to recite were met with laughter. My accent too thick. My accent too American. Twenty years later, in Los Angeles, I interrogate the shame I feel for being told that my accent is unmistakably Filipino.

The Ilustrado tames the beast.

Ninang asks me whose English is worse: "Your mom's or you dad's girlfriend's?" My family in Manila never lets a fault in English grammar go unnoticed. On a group chat with Lola, my aunts, and my two sisters, Ninang sends a screenshot of a message from my dad's girlfriend for us to laugh at.

What is the penance for our cruelty?

I am of my father's blood. I am of my mother's blood. I am of my father's blood. I am of my mother's blood. I am of my father's blood. I am of my mother's blood. I am of my father's blood. I am of my mother's blood. I am of my father's blood. I am of my mother's blood. I am of my father's blood. I am of my mother's blood. I am of my father's blood. I am

In the middle of a fight between my parents, I am held by my mother as my father smokes a cigarette inside their walk-in closet. "Your dad doesn't want me here." The room expands.

He says nothing.

                               There used to be something here.

"On settling in America, Kipling was determined to reinvent himself as a specifically American kind of writer, and for a while believed that his status as an outsider made him uniquely qualified to study American society."

                               You could have built a life here.

My father visits me in Los Angeles. It has been four months since I've been in the Philippines. As we make our annual drive to Canter's to pick up sandwiches, my father laments, "We could have built a life here."

The ex-pat laughs.

                               Tumahimik ka na.

At wag kang sumigaw, "Kalayaan"

I see a poster celebrating July 4 as Filipino-American Friendship Day. On it, the Philippine eagle and American bald eagle sit below the American and Philippine flags. The poster declares, "Let us celebrate the lasting friendship between our home countries."

Filipinos are known for their effusive hospitality.

Julián Felipe, the composer of the Philippine's national anthem, "Lupang Hinirang," based the melody on the Spanish national anthem, "Marcha Real"; the French national anthem, "La Marseillaise"; and "Grand March," from Giuseppe Verdi's *Aida*. Originally written in Spanish by Jose Palma, the lyrics were not translated into Tagalog until the 1940s. "Lupang Hinirang" translates to "chosen land." But barely anyone calls it that when they refer it to it, instead they pronounce the first line of the song: *Bayang magiliw*—gentle nation.

The history books say they saved us from the Spanish.

In *How to Hide an Empire,* Daniel Immerwahr writes, "One minute after the Spanish flag came down over Manila, an enormous U.S. flag climbed the flagpole in its place. The band struck up 'The Star Spangled Banner.'"

We're in our year-old home in the Philippines. A home built on inherited military land—

Fort Bonifacio, where my father's house is located, the house I return to when I go back to Metro Manila, both *was* and *is* a base for the Philippine army (the AFP):

- *Was* for where barracks might've been now stands an artificial city within a city.
- *Is* for the Sunday morning breakfast interruption of cannon tests.
- *Was* for the names of dead generals as street signs—one sign is named after Lola's father, General Cabal.
- *Is* for the street adjacent to the subdivision guardhouse selling military uniforms across from a 7-Eleven.
- *Was* for Lola's memories of American soldiers marching in a row when it was still called Fort William McKinley.
- *Is* for an area of the base, now a large real-estate property, called McKinley Hill.
- *Was* for Lolo, who once commanded the Philippine National Police.
- *Is* for the security checkpoints between Lawton Avenue—the road connecting my house to the artificial city—where the holster of a gun is in clear view.

The barrel extends beyond the image—

What's your last name?

Say it to be met with disbelief. Walang may pake.

General Imperial sits at the head of the dining table. Eighty, age spots stippled around his face, skin drooped, a full head of gray hair. He shouts to the maids to turn on the fan behind him, but there is no escaping the heat. He pulls a match from a box and lights another Marlboro Light. He was supposed to quit after his last hospital visit. He has gotten into the habit of smoking half the cigarette and then letting it burn on the ashtray. The ash falls onto the yellowed lace of the dining table cover. General Imperial runs out of cigarettes and commands one of the maids to buy him another pack. Members of his family pass him by, occasionally acknowledging his existence. They ask him how he's doing and leave when they tire of his answers. The bonsais he once tended rot in the front yard. An alarm on his phone reminds him it is sunset. It is time for him to stand up and get ready for mass. General Imperial—I call him Lolo

slaughters pigs

to feed them to you for dinner
and shows you their photos

before they are chopped on a platter. Each one had a name:
Princess, Porky, Pink. He took you

to his farm and showed off their pen. He let you
smell their shit. It covered everything. It was all

over their hooves and Lolo's shoes. He led you to a plot of
land a farm boy plowed whose name

you never found out. Stuck on the soles
of your shoes: mud and hay

you couldn't wait to wash off. You didn't think much of
that day. Lolo asks you about the Great

Books and turns tête-à-tête into vocabulary competition—
whosever language robs the other of precision gets

the most corpulent piece of meat. Is a name enough
to rid yourself of swine? Entrails simmer in a pot. A hair

juts out of the crispy chocolate
animal epidermis and swirls inside your mouth. *Masticated*:

the word Lolo used when you first chewed
the gummy tissue savory you hate that

you always crave for more

Tao'ng walang utang na loob

u-tang: hang / up / the / ph / one / means / i / can / not be re / trieved
/ sieve / through / bron / chi / tease / s out / to / xi / ci / ty / please
/ breathe / the / spir / it / out

ng: con / nects / neck / to / chest / strange / stains / in this / house /
found / ed / on / grad / ien / cy

lo-ob: knob / turns / left / left / door / op / en / stran /ger / caught /
me / peek / through / blinds / tries / a / sketch / out / of / e / lec
/ tric / al / wi / res / a / soul / coils / a / round / fruit / fall / en /
down / plas / tic / trees /

"Bakit dinukot niyo kami sa kadena?"

The syntax isn't right. I'm repeating myself again. What is the value of tautology?

"Bakit niyo dinukot kami sa kadena"
"Wag niyong dukutin kami sa kadena"
"Sa kadenang niyong dinukot"

I would rather go through tested systems.

"Ba't niyo dinukot kami sa kadena"

Lola entreats me to not bring up the past best forgotten.

"Bakit niyo kami dinukot sa kadena"

Return to the original: "Why brought ye us from bondage?"

what delight emerges
        from the echo of our dissonance   leave
                my breath suspended

on the tether of a buoy
        allow me another
                jubilant scream   before the whisper

sows vines into
        the unintelligible
                before the blooming, a riot—before the riot,
a pause—   how difficult to answer

        how something remains   :
                in the dream   I walk from dirt
field to dirt field to stumble onto dirt field

        a crowd   disperses
                at the sight of my arrival   a siren
gestures to sea   I find my head mid-collision
        the pointed front of a shipping vessel

                hungers for a new body   seeking escape
I learn what it means
        to turn away from—

                in the dream   I sing the suppurations
                of a text-to-speech machine
there must be a way out of here

                before the tendrils, a violence—

I translate Tagalog back into English:
"Why did you snatch us from our chains?"

                                        To protect his family
                                     from intruders, my father

                              lines the platform of the backyard walls
                              with spiraled barbed wire. My sister runs up

                                     the mango tree to win a game of hide
                                           and seek. Once found,
                                              my sister finds

                                         she must pry her foot
                                         from the fence. I use

                              this same image in another poem.

Ang madaling puri na hindi nananakit

I'm trying again.

Let's return to some sort of beginning.

My mother gathers my hair

and twists it into a bun, winding each strand
    in place. My scalp stretched. I try

to look for traces of myself
    in the mirror as she dabs powder

around swollen eyes. "You look just like me."
    A cat eats her kittens. The child's head

in her mouth. She understands survival
    as the faint cry of what was

once welcomed—Bone against bone
    in broad daylight, on subdivision sidewalk

as fur splinters palette. Young blood blossoms
    into a five-point star splayed across aging snout

as skull smashes into teeth. The first response: an ad
    for prosthetic limbs—Reattach the broken pieces

with gold, create surface. My mother inserts
    herself into the image of my siblings

on a beach in the Philippines, zoomed-in face
    beside portrait taken on steel sand. In a gallery,

pyramids of foil jut out from
    a black canvas, cutting my body

into—My mother wears a kaleidoscope
    of clothes my sister and I forgot

in her room. The foil carves
    each limb into triangulations—Behold

this bleeding, this splintered palette. My fingers
    count the squares on a map of the world to locate

a time zone. From the prime meridian,
    hours apart—I wander through the garden

to stomp on what Lola calls *shy plants*
    to watch dark green petals

clasp into each other, forming—Someone
    grabs my hand in the dark. A response:

the flinch, the body pulling away from—My mother
    tries to hold me while I sleep, curled up

against the beige walls of her bedroom as—I count squares
    toward the Philippines. I step on plants. I type N/A

on an information sheet. At a family dinner, Lolo
    reaches into his mouth

to pull false teeth. A formation: webs
    of saliva as frayed blue gums

smile. My mother tells me
    to stop crying. She leaves. Responds to memory:

I'm cutting it up, pasting it onto—I count
    enough squares toward California—the channels

change all at once. Barbara Walters reports the news
    while a clip of a tiger resting on a smiling cowboy's

shoulder plays on—I scribble *desire paths*
    on my palm. What appears:

a survey of the Southern California landscape
    displayed on a billboard. An infant

grips onto a finger. I peel bark off narra trees. My sister
    and I carve faces out from family photos. Excited

fingers misshaping the round surfaces
    of heads into rocky mountain paths. Glue oozes

from the in-between of my sister's face
    imposed on a wedding dress. A figure

in gaudy floral print as my enlarged
    toddler head cradles my infant brother.

We're laughing, passing it around—
    We cover our mother's face.

Ang sisi ng masmabuti

McKinley's Benevolent Assimilation Proclamation

EXECUTIVE MANSION, WASHINGTON

December 21, 1898

THE DESTRUCTION OF ███████████████ MANILA ██████

██

██

██████████████████████████████ *IS TO BE EXTENDED.*

██

██

██

██

██

██

████████████████████████████████████

████████ DUTY ████████████████████████████

██

████████████ SEVER███████████████████████

██

████ THE PERSONS ████████ THE PEOPLE OF ████████

████████████ RIGHTS AND RELATIONS ████████████

████████████ *WE COME*█████████████████ *TO*

PROTECT███████████████████████████████████

████████████ ALL PERSONS WHO███████████████

██████ CO-OPERATE WITH ████████████████████████

██

██

██

AUTHORITY, WHICH NECESSARILY IS AND MUST REMAIN SUPREME ████

ACCEPT THE SUPREMACY

ASSIMILATION

OVERCOME
THE PEOPLE

WILLIAM McKINLEY

and I crease my flesh

into concentric
tongues

writhing from the threat of holy
invasion   but the scabs

peel themselves onto the ground—crust spreads
enough   the air

mocks me. My place of worship is cool
when a gust sweeps out

the screaming. My place of worship
is the corrugated edges

of a cardboard box

filled with gaps
Am I extinction without struggle?

The text-to-speech machine will hiss

You descend from the wound of an indio child.
Galing ka sa dugo ng mga Espanol.
Kano.

Let us return to some sort of beginning. My last name.

Imperial.

Say it to be met with something resembling dignity.

yoursis
ahistoryof
beingsubdue
dyoursisahisto
ryofbeingsubdu
edyoursisahistory
ofbeingsubdu
edyoursisahistor
yofbeingsubd
edyoursisahi
storyofbein
gsu bdued y o
ur sisahis
toryofbeing subdue
d   your   sis ahisto
ryofbei   ng su   bdu
edyou   r   s isahist
oryof   b   ei
ngs   u   b   due d yoursis
ahist   o   ry   of be i ngsubd
ue   d   yours
isa   h   istoryofb e   ingsubdue
dyou   r   sisahist   o   ryofb eing
sub   d   uedyou rsisa hi st ory   of
being   s   u bdu ed you   rsisa h
istor   yofbein g sub d ued   yo
urs   isahist or yofbe   ing s
ubd   ue   dyour   sisah
istory   of b   e ingsu
bd   ue   d yoursisahi
s   toryofb eingsubduedyou
rsisahistoryofbeingsubdued
you rsisah istoryofbeingsubdue
dy ou r   sisahistoryofbeing
su   bduedyoursi sah
i   storyofbe   in
g   subduedyou r
sisahis   toryo fbe
in   g
s   u

Mine is a history   subdue the trouble in
the cadence of my speech fluctuating with each person
grineet ko beneath   the elongated vowels of a language i
must justify is mine na eyes na brown slanted they call me
a foreigner wherever i   am i trespasser kasi   since
my youth rather traitor with my private school grammar my
television inflection my speech means i am meant to
succeed i slept   with merriam-webster underneath
my pillow crinave ko ang ate cheerios when served rice sa
banana leaf the pollution smells of tangerines na   with
how i speak i reincarnate whatever hierarchy   over
and over the phone calls back   the swelling   distance of the
unanswered calls me back home still   questioning

                              what it means to belong ano ba

ang i thought i could be multitudes instead i listen to a Spanish family
in a Spanish home tell me how delicious Filipinos are alvarez says cook-
ies dark on the outside white on the inside are afraid halt in conversation self-deprecation tool
                    of consolation ito the shame of being
asked where are you from again and again

        from a constructed nation named after a european
king i am trying   to articulate what i love
        about the word bulbundukin   dito here again and
again pigilin mo 'yan
                          i remain   in the center
of crossfire balangiga bells ring finally returned back to a
history na your speech denies you   the privilege of any
home being home instead of where do i belong without
trembling to decide on one or the country both told to
privilege the blue passport na only mine na from a lineage
of war   for my blood is unmistakable for anything

other than filipino speak explain reincarnate the self
again and again for the palate of the other to belong to
crave for the sour tamarind soup manang cooked but afraid
na they will see the pancit canton appropriation of a culture
        am i allowed to claim as mine   my ex-girlfriend says
i rely too much   on the brown in my writing as if my
skin is a gimmick i decide   to put on dinuguan
pork blood stew dinugo to bleed to keep on bleeding
english   only school years in manila august for linggo ng
wika mother tongue quixotic
namamamaga   ang balat ko

      na i should be able to take it na when a drunk white
man mistakes me for bruce lee   do not fight retreat
      when a roommate asks how it is so easy for me to
assimilate sundo-sundo lang 'yan bahala na   asked where i
got my tan by feasting on lechon measuring the quality of
the pig by the crunch of its balat
                      grabe   she believes me
                 anything exotic believe me

        bahala na   let it be don't push for
understanding sometimes it doesn't have to mean anything
na   pigilin mo 'yan the white man will love your skin
for it is exotic gaugin carve my body into what it should be
again and again into decoration never into   subject it is
your skill   to be exhibited on white
museum walls   transform fracture of a narra tree let the
audience consume

brown bas relief release me from the imperial na

Ang daan na hindi malakaran,

A path I cannot tread,

A Portrait with My Grandmother
Escaping from Japanese Soldiers (1944)

the wagon / beside lola / when she is not yet / a lola / to anyone / who
has heard / this story / burst forth / wrinkled / lips / stay /

with me / we are rushed / through / de-fossilized / artillery slough /
backs against screeching / plywood draped in bamboo leaves / through
a tunnel / lola holds / her breath / / 'til / concrete / direct cuts / to sky /
no other / vision / to desire

but sky / sharp turn / left / lola rolls to corner / begs / / to go again / my
strained arm / retreats / where else / can the road lead / "hapon! hapon!"
/lola echoes

her mother / 's screaming /

                                        only memory can comfort me

Hagulgol ng tinatawanan ninyo

I spit at the mirror.
I hear a knock at the door.

Naririnig mo ba 'yan?

Hagulgol: the way grief bubbles
into heaving and demands it
be heard until
I force myself

It isn't the same. I've left something out.

to mistake it
for something close
to laughter

The poem is not in order.

Lola tells me a joke:

There were two birds

                                        Sigerepeat and sigerepot

Sigerepot flew away

                                                Who was left?

Sigerepeat

                                        There were two birds

Sigerepeat and sigerepot

                                        Sigerepot flew away

Who was left?

                                                Sigerepeat

There were   two birds

                Si   ge   re   peat and si   gerepot

Siger   epot   flew   away

Who   was   left?

                                        Si   ge   re   peat

There   were   two   birds

Si   ge   re   peat   and   si   ge   repot

                Sigerepot   flew   away

Who   was   left?

I don't know why she's laughing but she does and she repeats the joke I am four years old and I keep myself from crying and I don't know I am five years old and I don't know I am twelve years old and I don't know I am eighteen years old and I don't know and I don't know why it's funny it's like her other jokes the ones she tells me not to repeat because they're dirty like dikitdekat and I still don't get it but Lola laughs as she attempts to explain and I don't know why she keeps repeating herself but she laughs and I am nineteen and she says it slowly

I still don't understand.

"Say it with me, Christine."

Sige, repeat Sige, repeat

Sige, repeat after me.

The trouble is in the "P-E."

In the Philippines, the country of my birth,

I pronounce it as im-PEH-rial. The same "pe" in words such as pet, peck, petty, penetration, and petrified.

There is no escaping the obtrusive

rolling "r." In the US, the country of my citizenship,

I pronounce it as im-PEE-rial. The same "pe" in words such as peach, peel, peer, peace, and

Peoplepeoplepeoplepeoplepeoplepeoplepeoplepeoplepeoplepeoplepeo-
plepeoplepeoplepeoplepeoplepeoplepeoplepeoplepeoplepeoplepeople-
peoplepeoplepeoplepeoplepeoplepeoplepeoplepeoplepeoplepeoplepeo-
plepeoplepeoplepeoplepeoplepeoplepeoplepeoplepeoplepeoplepeople-
peoplepeoplepeoplepeoplepeoplepeoplepeoplepeoplepeoplepeoplepeo-
plepeoplepeoplepeoplepeople   peoplepeoplepeoplepeoplepeoplepeo-
plepeoplepeoplepeoplepeoplepeoplepeoplepeoplepeoplepeoplepeople-
peoplepeoplepeoplepeoplepeoplepeoplepeoplepeoplepeoplepeoplepeo-
plepeoplepeoplepeoplepeoplepeoplepeoplepeoplepeoplepeoplepeople-
peoplepeoplepeoplepeoplepeoplepeoplepeoplepeoplepeoplepeoplepeo

gather into lines	at immigration	and divide themselves
according to plastic		label fading
citizens/residents		foreign passports
open up		the first page
that's cool		your last name

I've left out the word "host."
So I look it up.
Nothing fits.

At the Girl's Home of the Manila Boystown Complex in Marikina, an orphanage where my university holds outreach programs to put its mission of solidarity with the poor into practice, I am a college freshman teaching preteen girls how to read in English. Only for today. I won't remember any of their names by the time I go back home. I won't even remember the name of the orphanage. I'll look it up online. I'll see if it fits into memory. I'll remember one thing—

"Ate, saan ka pumunta para sa grade school at high school?"

"Sa Miriam College."

"Kaya pala ang galing ng Ingles mo, Ate Christine!"

On the introduction of English as the language of instruction in the Philippines by American colonizers, Vicente Rafael, in his book *Motherless Tongues* writes, "On the one hand, students are unable to master the master's speech inasmuch as its sounds, references, and nuances remain outside of their experience."

I say, "Bakit, sinasabi mo 'yan?" when I want to say

"Why do you think that?"

I wonder if it is a matter of reputation. I wonder if that's what Miriam, the primary school I attended, is known for. In fifth grade, the teachers assigned English monitors to keep track of students who spoke in Filipino, meaning anything other than English. Any student caught speaking anything other than English had to pay a small fine. During recess, people began to speak in smaller circles so any slip of the tongue could be concealed. The English monitors never let their guard down. Even the sentence fillers like "na" and "palang" wouldn't escape their ears.

Rafael continues, "On the other hand, they have lost their capacity to speak their mother tongue, which has been forbidden to them."

I never worried. I never got caught. I never spoke in anything other than English. I was resentful I wasn't assigned to be an English monitor.

One of the girls takes the thickest book from the shelf and places it on the table for me to see. The book is red. She points to its title:

The Merriam-Webster Dictionary

My companion nudges my shoulders and turns away to keep her laughter from being heard.

Rafael continues, "Overcoming the 'handicap' of translation meant making the foreign familiar rather than merely fearsome, taming it into an instrument of one's thoughts and a ready servant of one's expression."

I will recall this moment during dinner with my family and we will laugh. I will recall this memory years later, in Los Angeles, and question what it means to feel pride.

Sige, repeat.

Lolo tells me a joke about a Filipino in America eating at a diner for the first time:

A Filipino sits down at the diner and grabs a menu. The American waiter comes to his table. The Filipino orders his entrée. The American says,

> "That comes with soup or salad."
> "Yes," the Filipino responds.
> "So, soup or salad?"
> "Yes," the Filipino responds.
> "Sir, do you want the soup or salad?"
> "Yes, I will have the super salad."

The Filipino responds.

My family and I laugh.

"Filipinos Are Smiling a Lot More According to Latest Gallup World Happiness Index"

—*Good News Pilipinas*

"New Survey Shows Americans Are Unhappier Than They've Been in Years: There's a Potentially Surprising Reason Why"

—*Vox*

"What Immigrants Know about Happiness": "The act of migration involves taking risks in pursuit of meaningful reward and having faith in the future. Everyone should try to live more like that."

—*The Atlantic*

I want to be happy. Give me a method.

"How to be Happy. Filipino American."

—*Kuya Vic* blog

"The Funny in the Filipino: Are Filipinos Trying to Escape Our Country's Harsh Realities through Humor?"

—*Rappler.com*

"Survey: American Happiness Reaches 50-Year Low"

—*Futurity.com*

"Immigrants to the US Are Happier Later in Life Than Natives—Despite Generally Being Worse Off Financially": "Give me your tired, your poor, your huddled masses yearning to breathe free."

—*ZME Science*

In Kipling's poem, "host" is a euphemism for captive. The colonizer humors the host. The host humors the guest. Observe the customs. Eat their food. Let the rituals be performed. Let them howl. Let them think they are being listened to. Let them

welcome you

In recent years, many expats have experienced why "It's More Fun in the Philippines."

inside the house I am taught to call home.

I don't know where things are anymore.

To keep the house in order, my father relies on Manang Lita. I hesitate to say "maid." I learn not to say "yaya" anymore. Manang Lita, whom my siblings and I called Yaya Manang for the first two years of her employment, knows where everything should be. I hear my father ask for his pinstripe Hugo Boss trousers and she returns with them perfectly creased. I hear my sister ask for her dog's leash and Manang instructs the houseboy to fetch it from the garden. I hear my brother ask for his soccer cleats and Manang asks which ones and reminds him that they're in the car and he's about to leave. I hear Manang dry heaving in the backyard. I hear Manang is in the hospital. I hear Manang bought a house in the province. I hear Manang leave as my father's lover moves my childhood books from shelves in the attic into cardboard boxes by the foyer. My father's lover takes the photographs with my mother in them and puts them in cardboard boxes in the attic. My father's lover takes my sheets and puts them on my father's bed. My father's lover wants the inside of the house painted blue. My father's lover drinks all the wine in the glass cupboards. My father's lover hits a button to call the maids up to my father's room. My father's lover instructs the maids to no longer use my younger siblings' bathroom. My father's lover calls my father "baby." My father's lover calls herself a stepmom. My father's lover speaks English like my mother, and Lola and I laugh whenever her grammar slips. My father's lover doesn't know how to use possessive pronouns. My father's lover speaks in what she thinks is an English accent. My father's lover sends another manang away. My father's lover keeps my father company. I don't want to hear her call this house a home.

I don't know where things are.

Nasaan na? Yabang-yabang! Madamot pa!

I wonder what belongs to me?

Why do I care? I'm not there.

Sa lahat mong iniwan at gawa,

All you've left and done.

Sa lahat mong iniwan. Sa lahat mong ginawa.

"Why do you care? You're not here."

Payton asks, "Why do you care?"

     When I tell Payton that the waiter handed her the check / is surprised I'm paying for the check, she insists:

     "You're too paranoid. You think everyone is out to get you."

She tells me I'm not her usual type. That's why I'm special.

                       "Ay, ang puti niya!"

     We talk about our travels to different countries. As we do, she never fails to mention how foreigners tell her that she is too beautiful to be Filipino.

My mother reminds me not to forget to pack papaya whitening soap for her and her relatives.

     "Ay, ang ganda niya and laging naka-smile!"

Ninang asks, "Why do you still love her? What's so special about her? She's just a white girl with a flat nose."

     Payton laughs as I speak in Tagalog.

Lola pinches the skin of my nose to sharpen its contours. "Para mas-matulis pagtanda mo," which translates to "So we can sharpen the bone."

     Again, Payton holds my arm up against the sun of my bedroom window and raises it up to call attention to how dark my hands are against hers. "We're like yin and yang."

     She laughs. I laugh too.
I need the line break.

I'm not writing while

"Rectify the flesh."

I'm with Payton unless I'm writing about her.

"Can you write a novel about me? I don't get your poems."

"Mimesis, as with all desire, falters."

As we look at photographs of us taken in Hong Kong, Payton notices how overjoyed I look. She notices our height difference. She notices the languid smile on her face beside my goofy, overexcited grin makes it appear as if I'm taking a photo with a celebrity.

My mother asks if Payton is a model.

I don't know if this is a pose.

Sinasabi nila swerte ako.

When we're standing, I'm always looking up at her.

My toes ache from tip-toeing.

Masaya ka?

Lola says she can't imagine Payton without a smile on her face. She says I should be more like her.

I want to be happy.

Payton sings a song I wrote her back to me.

I'm counting the days until I move to LA.

"I hate when you're so hard on yourself."

I keep two time zones displayed on my phone.

> Over FaceTime, I half-jokingly ask Payton to move to LA, and her tone shifts, "It's not that easy for me. I can't just go wherever I want."

A relative says he's tired of how the victimhood narrative of Black people proliferates the media. He says it's like if all I talked about was colonialism.

> After Payton reads a poem of mine, she calls me up. "I just think people who keep putting brown in their writing are parang a gimmick, you know? Like we get it, you don't have to keep talking about it."

I'm twelve years old, rubbing the skin of my armpit with a loofa, thinking force will make it lighter.

> She presses her head onto my chest on the way to the airport. I'm moving to LA. The tears dry onto my shirt and cloak my cologne. I like how much she's holding on.

It's so much easier to write about surrendering control. It's so much easier to be okay with incapability in the poem.

> The memory of watching Payton

> kiss someone, someone tall, someone white, someone desirable

No one is victim here. No one wants to be.

in a dark nightclub floods me with dread. The memory of her telling me that she wanted to prove she was still attractive to others while being with me.

Does it make you feel resilient to be this ugly monster of regret?

"You need to stop thinking about it! It happened. What do you want?

On the television, the president brandishes a clenched fist.

You stayed."

Lola tells me about the day she realized she wanted to leave Lolo.

I hear my father whisper,

"We could've built a life here."

2003. The year my mother leaves for Los Angeles. She hasn't left yet. The middle of summer. The house gradually becomes emptier and emptier. The giant television in the den. The green recliner in my parent's room. The extra freezer in the garage. The black Toyota van by the gate. They all vanish. My mother comes home less and less. JP and Camille, three years old and one year old, respectively, sleep with the maids. Casey, six years old, cuts the hair of her Barbies because she's tired of how they look. She doesn't ask for new toys. My father barely speaks.

We're broken up. Payton has moved out of my? our? studio apartment. We're inside her new apartment, smoking cigarettes on a mattress, while my dog sleeps in the corner.

It's almost like before until I remember.

2003. The beginning of summer.

To heal the wound, one must refrain from contact.

My parents take Casey and me out for dinner. This is the first time in months. My parents are barely in the same room anymore. But now, it's just like before. Almost like Folsom. They take us to California Pizza Kitchen. We are in Manila. I douse my pepperoni pizza in parmesan cheese. Casey recalls the time I slammed the bottle so hard the lid fell off. We laugh. My parents don't notice. They don't speak. And then they do. And then their voices rise. There's no escape. We arrive home. Voices rise. My parents send Casey and me to our rooms. My baby siblings are asleep in the maids' room. Again. A muffled scream is still a scream. Casey wakes up. I am eight years old. Already tired—

Kneeling outside my parent's room and knocking on their door.

"The mirror. Does she know how much that costs?"

there used to be something here there used to be something here there
used to be something here there used to be something here there used
to be some-   t h i n g
here   there   used to be
something   here   there
used to be   something
here   there   used to be
something   here   there
used to be   something
here   there   used to be
something   here   there
used to be   something
here   there   used to be
something   here   there
used to be   something
here   there   used   to
be   some-   t h i n g
here   there   used to be
something   here   there
used to be   something
here   there   used to be
something   here   there
used to be   something
here   there   used to be
something here there used to be something here there used to be
something here there used to be something here there used to be
something here there used to be something here there used to be
something here there used to be something here there used to be
something here there used to be something here there used to be
something here there used to be something here there used to be some-
thing here there used to be something here there used to be some-
thing here there used to be something here there used to be something
here there used to be something here there used to be something here
there used to be something here there used to be something here there
used to be something here there used to be something here there used

this is a photograph of my mother and father kneeling in a cathedral during their wedding something I cannot call my own "It's happening again" I imagine this is a promise of metaphor the same hands tangle remembering thrashing the room impenetrable let me in splinter this is a photograph taken before shouting this is a totem to collapse only possible with contact line the house with barbed wire line doorways with insecticide "Nothing can get in" until nothing wants to get in anymore my father instructs "Put it in storage" this is a renovation not renewal not wanting to come back it promised to be ululating joy mistaken for madness bleached perforations from exposure to light puncture impulse to turn away from the specifics of a bedtime story "It's happening again" of a first meeting my mother and father framing destiny as family "Store it in the attic"

Ninang, my father's eldest sister, calls my father up. This is not my memory. This is what I have been told. Earlier in the day, my mother went to the family office to request access to my father's shares in the family company. "No, Mel." My mother, ever the rapacious consumer of Filipino soap operas responded,

"Sister ka lang! Ako yun asawa ni John!"

Sa lahat mong iniwan. Sa lahat mong ginawa.

Everything you've left.
Everything you've done.
In the white space of
translation, the debris accumulates.

My mother insists she and my father would still be together if it weren't for the distance.

Boarding a plane back to Manila, a stranger asks why my siblings and I look so sad. "We're going back to the Pinas! Smile for da' [sic] motherland!"

I don't know which language this statement was spoken in. This is not my memory. This is what I've been told. Ninang calls my father up. "John, if you can't take it anymore, you tell me, okay?"

To stop Casey and I from fighting, Lola sings,

All that you've left continues to live on without you.

"Sisters, sisters
There were never such devoted sisters."
Payton says she doesn't understand my devotion to my family.

My father and I are watching TV in his room. We do this a lot. I catch him lying down on the same side of the bed he has lain in for twenty years as he looks for something to watch, a glass of whiskey in hand; I lie on the empty space of the bed and take the glass from him to drink from it. We're watching TV and drinking whiskey in my father's room. I pull my left leg toward me. My dad laughs. He instructs me to raise my leg upward as he raises his. "Our legs are like carbon copies of each other." Our calves bulge out like knolls.

My mother claims I am the spitting image of my father in his mid-twenties. My mother claims she sees so much of him in me.

     We're broken up. My brother sings a song to make me laugh.

     "Payton flies over the ocean / Payton flies over the sea / Payton flies over the ocean / So bring back Payton . . ." He keeps going. He doesn't stop until I'm not laughing anymore.

To keep out intruders, my father lines the house with barbed wire fence.

     I ask Payton where my apartment keys are. Lola tells me to change the locks.

To keep out my mother, my father instructs me to place a credit freeze.
                      "Why do you care?"

Do not stall the line. Keep it moving.

     Memory does not exist to comfort anyone.

In the dream, I can't stop running.

                      You're not here."

Repetition compulsion: "the desire to return to an earlier state of things."

Richard Siken, in his poem "Litany in Which Certain Things Are Crossed Out," writes, "You see, I take the parts that I remember and stitch them back together / to make a creature that will do what I say / or love me back."

My mother says, "I couldn't stand Payton. She was a bitch." I find myself wanting to defend her. I let my mother keep going.

The last time I see my mother in the Philippines, I am waving to her from the passenger seat of my father's car. Not understanding the emergence of tears.

Duwag ka! No one here is victim. No one wants to be.

I remember writing a poem to Payton: "my sunken body majestic / in your light"

I struggle to translate the line "all ye leave or do."

Duwag. Ang dami mong gusto. Ang dami mong kasalanan. Do not stall the line.

I remember asking her how she could be so selfish. I remember her response:

"What? I'm happy."

I want to remember not wanting I want to remember not wanting I
want to remember not wanting I want to remember not wanting
I want to remember not wanting I want to remember not wanting I
want to remember not wanting I want to remember not wanting
I want to remember not wanting I want to remember not wanting I want to remember not wanting I want to remember not wanting I want to remember not wanting I want to remember not wanting

to leave

Where?

Lola asks

Mom asks

"Kailan ka babalik dito?"

I don't know

                                                      "When will you be back?"

how to stop regurgitating the diction
of empires spawns cobwebs
from the cries of its captives.

Ang hagulgol ng mga bihag mo

The poem is not in order.

I'm back to translation again. I do away with host.

The cries of your captives.

I am learning

to be less grateful. "What is your last name?"

As if it mattered.   Say it to be met
with disbelief.   So I return

to the origin: from the Latin: *imperium*—command,

authority, empire. From Spanish. From Portuguese.

    From whatever comes   to pass.

                              I am not supposed to·be

what is birthed

              from the abstract

                              I hear the ex-pat laugh.

Mounds of rubble gather—

('Yan dahan-dahan)   **sa banal na liwanag**
: to be slow, to be careful

when I jam my tongue
in between

the metal railing of the balcony
collecting all that had been

trapped and carrying it
inside me

A Common Characteristic of Tagalog is the Repetition of a Word

- For emphasis

  o A rudimentary example, such as *Karga-karga niya yun mga bagahe*
    - *Karga niya yun mga bagahe*, would translate to *She/they/he carries the bags.*
    - Karga-karga augments the sentence.
      □ Literally translates to *carry-carry*
      □ How does the repetition of *karga* function in the sentence? Instead, maybe, what does it do?
        ◆ It may heighten the affective quality of the word. The carrying is not a neutral act in this regard. There is something in the way the bags are carried that demands someone take notice.
  o This use of repetition may suggest a kind of seeing through the performativity of one's action. *Karga-karga* as if the bags they/he/she are carrying aren't heavy or need not be carried. The subject carrying the bags, the speaker of the sentence suggests, could be doing something more noteworthy, something more useful with their time. It may also suggest *play*.
    - A classic example: *bahay-bahay/bahay-bahayan* (an addition of **-an** we will return to later),
      □ translates literally to *house-house.*
        ◆ In other words, *the semblance of a house.* Does that make sense?
      □ Let's use it in a sentence, *Maglaro tayo ng bahay-bahay*, which translates to *Let's play house-house.*
        ◆ In other words, *Let's play the resemblance of a house.*
          ◇ In other words, *let's pretend.*
  o However, if the first karga were to be appended with an **-ng**—*kargang-karga*—this would emphasize the ease and competency by which the action is executed.

- *Kargang-karga niya yun bagahe* literally translates to *Carrying carrying he/she/they the bags,* in other words,
- No, that's not right either. The tone of the sentence, as modified by *really,* can be read in different ways; I will limit myself
  - to two of these ways:
    - one being sarcastic
    - the other admiring.
- Another means of repetition for emphasis is the insertion of **ng** between two identical verbs: *Karga ng karga.* Here **ng** works similar to the **-ing** suffix of the present participle in English.
- These were examples for verbs; for an adjective such as *sira,* which translates to broken/cut-off, the repetition of *sira,* resulting in *sirang-sira,*
  - translates to ***broken-broken***.
    - In other words, *Really broken.*
      - *Sobrang sira*
        - *Soooo broken*
          - *Sirang-sira!*
  - Which translates to
    - *ayos*, which translates to *fix* (as verb) or *fixed* (as adjective).
      - *Ayos-ayos* would literally translate into *fix-fix.*
      - *Ayos-ayos,* which as we noted earlier with *karga,* which means to *carry/bear,* has a performativity to the action or a perceived performativity to the action that is used against the speaker.
        - E.g, *Ayos-ayos ka diyan, pero wala.*
          - Which literally translates to *Fixing-fixing you there, but nothing you show,* and might mean *You keep fixing, but you have nothing to show for it,* which might translate to *Patuloy kang nagaayos, ngunit walang bunga,* which might translate to *You con-*

tinue fixing, yet it yields no fruit, which might translate to

❏ *It's really broken. Can't fix it,* which translates to

♦ *Talagang sira. Hindi-maayos,* which might translate to

◊ *Sira, talaga. Di-maayos,* which translates to,

› *Broken, really broken. Can't be fixed,* which might translate to

o *Sira, sirang-sira. 'Di 'yan maayos.*

▪ It's like when you're asked *Where are you from,* and you respond *here* or a city in whatever country you're in and they respond with *But where are you **from** from,"* which translates to *Saan ka ba galing, **talaga**?*

❏ *Talaga* translates into English as *really,* which can be

♦ an expression of disbelief, e.g., *Really?!*

♦ an adverb used to emphasize (maybe even exaggerate) the authenticity of something, e.g., *It was **really** funny,*

◊ which might translate to *talagang nakakatawa,*

◊ which literally translates to *really laughter inducing.*

❏ What if you answer with *I don't know,*

♦ which translates to *Hindi ko alam,* which would literally translate as

♦ *No me know,* in other words,

♦ *I don't know,*

♦ *Hindi ko alam,* which

◊ (I think)

◊ literally translates to *I am not knowledge.*

› But the question could also just be asking, *Where did you come from?*

› That sounds like the same question,

o an expression of confirmation, e.g., *Were you really there?* "Really," which translates to

- *Nandiyan ka ba talaga.* "Talaga," which translates to
  - *Are you really there?* "Yes."
    - ♦ Which translates to *Nandiyan ka ba?* "Oo."

I am five years old, sitting behind my Lola's seat in our family's gray Toyota van, when she asks me what her name is. I answer, "Lola." Ninang, her eldest daughter, is in the car with us. They laugh. I don't understand why. Everyone calls her Lola. "Lola is not my name. My name is Maria Aurora. 'Lola' is 'grandma.' Your Mama Rose is your Lola in the States.

I am your Lola here."   I exclaim,

"You're my Lola, Lola!"

Really/talaga, which translates to "I am proving allegiance."

Imantsa mo ng nabubuhay
At imantsa ng patay

where do I turn to in the hours of reckoning
      the seed pods of snapdragons resemble skulls
          wailing   I sift memory 'til the image
            the first brush with carcass
   is a still   from a movie
   I can' t remember
      on land my father bought
         the low-tide   exposes ruin
 volcanic eruption   :   a symphony of craters
    I take photos to fixate on
        later when the time is right   later
 when I pretend
    the icecaps still have time
    to melt   what on earth cannot be
called a cemetery

Lola texts: "the internet is my salvation"
      "are u busy?
      "Went to dinner with your siblings"
      "I know youre busy"
      "Ay Chrisatine, don't worry!"
      "Don't tell anyone. I have fever!!!"
      "I finished a new show on Netflix nanaman"
      "Taking the day off. Sleepy ako!"
      "So proud of you"

I lullaby
            the castanets   of her brittle bones
                        to convince myself she won't die
                        I pluck beads
            from a rosary that figures itself
                        divine in the tungsten light
                                    there's always allowance
for error   but not on the form

I don't want to fixate
            on the pullulating cracks of
                        her nicotine skin   orchestrates the shock

                        I know I've heard before
            I know I can't remember   the last time I wept
                        so hard I focused
            on the shrinking   wool of my sweater
                        when the mirror fogs   I see myself
                        return to penance pleading

"Let's be still"

so they don't die

I hope

Lola keeps all the flowers I send her

in the freezer—

My mother makes up memories when she recounts her life in the Philippines and doesn't want to be corrected by me

again nanaman naririnig ko yun mga butas ng salita niya

                      the television white noise dictates
                      something resembling silence

I hear it expelled from my brother's mouth   "Mom lies a
lot, 'di ba" my mother tells my brother

                   you will always come from a womb

about how she let no one else hold him but her

"I don't remember Mom, but I remember sleeping beside the yayas with
Camille   every night and in the morning she and I would cry
if we woke up without someone between us"   may naganap
dito na walang may alam   walang may alam walang may alam walang
may

my mother writes e-mails I copy-paste
into Google to see whose language she calls her own

              the blueprint of a tongue is a crossfire

again and again the swelling distance ano ang inuulit mo dito here again
                  it halts me enough to bleed

and again I confront my mother   I know why she left the Philippines.

She responds,

"There's a quote from Instagram—" Please stop.

Please stop.
Please stop.
Please stop.
Please—

"There's a quote from Instagram that goes 'People will only remember you for your faults and not for your good deeds.'"

And I laugh

When I read Kipling
to translate   "(Ah slowly) to the light"

"('Yan dahan-dahan) diretso sa liwanag."

Sinasalin ko ang dusa na hindi ako sigurado na pwede kong kargahin:

I translate a burden I will never be sure is mine/my own/mine to call my
own: to carry

Where can we turn (to for) definition

hi-rap: the / I / not / like / hi / but / hee / breathe / squeeze / the / breath / ing / wraps / the / la / rynx / like / a / rid / dle / sphinx / the / an / swer / too / hard / the / an / swer / on / hold / on / or

tu-long: cor / rect / my / wrongs / for / too / long / i / heard / on / ly / soft / coughed / out / son / nets / at / a / for / eign / pace / pa / tience

lu-pit: or / lu / pit / not / ip / it / re / peat / ed / stuck / too / hard / on / dif / fer / ence / de / fer / ence / phy / si / cal / ly / e / du / cat / ed / kow / tow

ta-o: not / tao / but / two / syl / la / bles / bounc / ing / a / round / like / chil / dren / sound / ing / out / vow / els / to / re / hearse / real / words

pa-sen-sya: na / un / cle / when / he / land / ed / in / los / an / ge / les / less / con / fi / dent / had / to / pause / a / brupt / make / way / for / where / na/palang/diba / would / be / placed / / in / ab / sence

si-gaw: not / all / owed / to / shout / counts / back / ward / from / one / thou / sand / to / sand / down / im / pul / sing / o / ver / some / thing / un / named

bu-lol: lo / la / keeps / a / gainst / threat / of / los / ing / an / oth / er / called / out / of / a / cu / bi / cle / in / L / A / long / dis / tance / call / a / bout / mo / ther / can't / cry / be / tween / err / ands / in / the / car / tongue / un / knott / ed / / swal / lows / what / calls / it / self / fe / ral / wail

sa-li-ta: i / mutt / er / my / noise / an / noys / me / turns / red / turn / e / ver / y / thing / in / in / dif / fe / rence / i / m / plode

saan 'to galing? Saan 'to galing?

Again, I retranslate my Tagalog:
(Yes, careful) into the holy light.

da-han-da-han: what / words / can / not / grasp / can / not / re / main /
must / hol / low / space / gaps / on / to / which / fin / gers / fold

There is no chronology to the poem.
Kipling, what responsibility do I have

to you? I skip the line about Egypt. It doesn't mean anything to me. It doesn't make sense. It doesn't fit.

Who am I to continue?
Who are we to return?

Bakit niyo kami dinukot sa kadena

Do you remember?
Are you paying attention?
Why did you snatch us from our chains?

Itapos ang araw pambata

Again, it isn't right.
That's no excuse.

Tapusin ang mga araw ng kabataan mo
Translates to: finish the days of your youth

Or at least I hope it does.

Payton demands to know why

I am so adamant

she no longer go to the family house—the house I spend holidays in,
the house I grew up in, the house I was taught to call home, the house

I never hesitated to call home—

Beeping

signals arrival. Rusty blue gate. Creaking. Needs to be oiled up.
Needs to be repaired. Blue arch above strewn with vines. Dog
escapes. Bonsai falls down. Cracked pot. Fractals of soil. Slanted
driveway escapes into the garage. Cracked asphalt floor. The smell
of burnt chorizo.

"Please stop. I don't feel safe knowing you're there."

Sinong binabantayan mo? Ano'ng binabantayan mo? Ha?

Translates to host.   Who can swear they belong?

An altar adorned with figurines of Santo Niño and Mama Mary
adjacent to the small white gate leading into the basement. Closets filled with old comic books. Closets filled with dusty dresses.
Maids' quarters adjacent to a mausoleum of a retired general's
memorabilia. Badges. Dusty rifles. An unchecked leak. A renovated
room. Petrichor.

"Why does it matter? You're not here."

Gumigising ka sa silaw ng ibang bansa.

Why should I care?

The room that was once mine in Lolo's house is used as storage.

The room I call my own in my father's house is never slept in.

I empty out the room my mother insists I can claim is mine in her rented house in El Monte.

I recall the flood.

Lola moves out of Lolo's house

Kabisado mo 'to.

in 2009 after Typhoon Ondoy. Lola does not want to be there for another flood

Where do you call home?

I recall the flood.

My father drives
to the store to buy a raft to rescue

        family in my grandparents' house half submerged sitting
     by lanai no contact since seven last night we heard it was water
        rising obscuring surface first floor i once ran in the dark to
                                     stave off

rising and rising from below cigarette butts thrown by my cousins in
cardboard box in basement does water pierce closed windows what
floats among splinters of glass rising and right my father returns to tell
me of the man who pleaded

        buy his raft his wife his infant child his hands holding bills
                                  for my father

to refuse i alone in my room ctrl + r the news refresh feed information
accumulating

                  as rescue for all i know is what I see

a woman cradles two children on her roof on a house images replay the
raft of medusa who can stand all this water who is there left to save

        on my bed on the second floor of a three-story house only
                hearing drizzle if only I could listen

the undulation of sewage water waves pinch disaster between fingers
and save Lola

                    are your portraits swimming?

Am I ever where I'm supposed to be?

Kargahin mo ang dusa ng puti

Hindi ka ba, nasasawa.

                                    Sawa: to be sick of

A poem is nothing but its form.

                  I want to say "hawa" but use "infect" instead.

Hawa: to make sick

                  In a poem, I write: "Rhyme is all revision."

MacArthur reassures the Filipinos he will return.

                  I want to return to the present.

I stare at the chains dangling from the frame of Luna's *Spoliarium.*

                  Lolo wheezes through an oxygen mask.

The ex-pat laughs.

                  May namatay dito.

Lola insists we make a pilgrimage to MacArthur's statue in Bohol.

                  Nothing fits. So I turn experience into metaphor.

Walang kasya. Masyadong maluwag.

                  "You're wasting your time. Get back to work."

Before I knew what "immigrant" meant.

                  Masaydong mahigipit.

How does one translate "heavy harness"?

Wala: asked where I feel most at home.

I was born in Mandaluyong City, Manila, Philippines, in 1994.
"A howling wilderness."

"Dayuhan ay nahalina."

An ambulance stalls in traffic.

I am born a US citizen.

Why do you care? You aren't here.

Walang ginto sa tula.

The artifact is being restored.

"If I should die before I wake, I pray the Lord my soul to take."

"Hoy! Kaya kita tinawag. Ingles ng Ingles! Ang sosyal naman."

A line from a movie: "Each time life breaks the circle, the games turn gray and ridiculous."

Ang gaspang ng hangin.

Gaspang → Lola spreads moisturizer on my elbow and warns it will darken.

Before I knew what an ex-pat was.

I dream of pulling a scorpion from my palm.

Kipling, are you there?

Tumatawa lang sila.

My mother meets a stranger and rewrites her history again.

Kipling tries out a different tongue.

Didn't you ask for this?

Ginusto mo 'to, 'di ba?

Dual nationality by automatic operation of different laws rather than by choice For example a child born in a foreign country to US national parents may be both a US national and a national of the country of birth Or an individual having one nationality at birth may naturalize at a later date in another country and become a dual national If you are a former Filipino that does not want to or cannot apply for dual citizenship but want to click here stay in the Philippines longer than allowed by the visa waiver agreement you can do the following Apply for a visa Check for the visa that you can apply for here Please check first with your foreign country of birth/naturalization if it allows dual citizenship click here A US citizen may naturalize in a foreign state without any risk to Natural-born Filipinos who lost their Filipino citizenship through naturalization in a foreign country may re-acquire Philippine citizenship by taking the Philippine Oath of Allegiance before a duly authorized Philippine official Dual nationals owe allegiance to both the United States and the foreign country required to obey the laws of both countries and either country has the right to enforce US law does not mention dual nationality or require a person to choose one nationality or The Philippine Oath of Allegiance does not require a person to renounce his allegiance to any other country click here find additional information on dual nationality and the potential challenges for international travelers here click here In order to relinquish US nationality by virtue of naturalization as a citizen of a foreign state the law requires your cooperation do not create proof that either or both parents will claim the above circumstances the person is a dual citizen by birth and need only to comply with complete requirements for Intent may be shown by the person's statements and conduct to become a US citizen click here is one of the most important decisions in an individual's life a person born outside of the United States may acquire Filipino Mother a person born outside of the United States may become a US citizen and that person shall please click here applicant be assessed using only military ID The following conditions have been met

Someday, I will receive the earth as it floats above me.
Saan ka babalik?
Someday, I will receive the earth as it floats above me.
Saan ka babalik?
Someday, I will receive the earth as it floats above me.
Saan ka babalik?
Someday, I will receive the earth as it floats above me.
Saan ka babalik?
Someday, I will receive the earth as it floats above me.
Saan ka babalik?
Someday, I will receive the earth as it floats above me.
Saan ka babalik?
Someday, I will receive the earth as it floats above me.
Saan ka babalik?
Someday, I will receive the earth as it floats above me.
Saan ka babalik?
Someday, I will receive the earth as it floats above me.
Saan ka babalik?
Someday, I will receive the earth as it floats above me.
Saan ka babalik?
Someday, I will receive the earth as it floats above me.
Saan ka babalik?
Someday, I will receive the earth as it floats above me.
Saan ka babalik?
Someday, I will receive the earth as it floats above me.
Saan ka babalik?
Someday, I will receive the earth as it floats above me.
Saan ka babalik?
Someday, I will receive the earth as it floats above me.
Saan ka babalik?
Someday, I will receive the earth as it floats above me.
Saan ka babalik?

Kapaghinawakan ang lumulutang lupa, manatili ka muna.
Where do you call home?
Kapaghinawakan ang lumulutang lupa, manatili ka muna.
Where do you call home?
Kapaghinawakan ang lumulutang lupa, manatili ka muna.
Where do you call home?
Kapaghinawakan ang lumulutang lupa, manatili ka muna.
Where do you call home?
Kapaghinawakan ang lumulutang lupa, manatili ka muna.
Where do you call home?
Kapaghinawakan ang lumulutang lupa, manatili ka muna.
Where do you call home?
Kapaghinawakan ang lumulutang lupa, manatili ka muna.
Where do you call home?
Kapaghinawakan ang lumulutang lupa, manatili ka muna.
Where do you call home?
Kapaghinawakan ang lumulutang lupa, manatili ka muna.
Where do you call home?
Kapaghinawakan ang lumulutang lupa, manatili ka muna.
Where do you call home?
Kapaghinawakan ang lumulutang lupa, manatili ka muna.
Where do you call home?
Kapaghinawakan ang lumulutang lupa, manatili ka muna.
Where do you call home?
Kapaghinawakan ang lumulutang lupa, manatili ka muna.
Where do you call home?
Kapaghinawakan ang lumulutang lupa, manatili ka muna.
Where do you call home?
Kapaghinawakan ang lumulutang lupa, manatili ka muna.
Where do you call home?
Kapaghinawakan ang lumulutang lupa, manatili ka muna.
Where do you call home?

The child has at least click here one parent Hence, the loss, mutilation or destruction of their minor children physically present can do the following upon reaching the age of an oath of allegiance may be shown by the person's statements and conduct does not allow persons to avoid possible Renunciation click here A child of having to perform any act to acquire or perfect the services that best suits the form outlying possession her latest History and Genealogy are not subject to income taxes country click here It is important to note the problems attendant to dual nationality In accordance with laws that prohibit dual nationality derived from sources in conflict with the laws of the other Use of the foreign passport you may be forced to click here translate the foreign currency into a US passport into the parents are not married unless deceased The father acknowledges responsibility as the mother may hamper efforts of dependents not physically present a child content is not inconsistent A child that is a derivative click here dual citizen must be required to obey laws If the mother is required at birth, and after birth click here A child an alien renounce US citizen mother protection as not inconsistent integrity as subject to currency as outside the laws of the Philippines as a US citizen as physically present as representative as submission of copy as within and without authorization as wishes to retain as jurisdiction as Family as prior residence as currency as child click here by automatic operation of A person may also want to stay certified as A person as a generally derivative process acquires any risk born in accordance with click here provisions and conditions that existed at the time of the person's birth unless deceased the name as appearing as Genealogy as a return as more information you must click here consider the naturalization of reasonable time is required to enter and leave the public domain unless otherwise when all of the following conditions have been met If you cannot click here if you cannot comply with click here modes of compliance click here you must

translate click here

How long does jetlag last?

My mother asks if the mirror remains.

Manatili ka muna. Manatili ka.

An article from *The New Yorker* titled "Rudyard Kipling in American" reads, "In later years, Kipling never discouraged readers from finding in the Jungle Books a political allegory. In one interpretation, the Law of the Jungle is the Raj, and the Monkey People are the hapless Indians whom the British came to civilize. Or, Kipling also suggested, you could see the Monkey People as an indictment of American populists, and

their habit of promising everything

accomplishing nothing."

Matalim pero matamis na karangunan,
Literally translates
to "Penetrating yet sweet that is call," in other words
"Penetrating yet sweet call," in other words
"Matulis ngunit tamis na tawag," in other words
"Sharp but sweet calls" from

my mother left me in doubt of recall
    my father lets rust grow on the barbed wire fence
in the backyard of the house he and my mother built
    I play "bahay-bahay"
inside forts made of blankets collecting dust
    inside my parents' closet my siblings and I open up
drawers to find batteries for the remote
    visitors welcome visitors welcome
to the dream where I am running from dirt field to Lola
    scratches the itch on my back as the television
vanishes in the living room I fashion a shatter
    if the house I was certain
was home the day I arrived in Manila
    not knowing what not to say
sweating inside a dark room ossifies
    into my parents place me in between their bodies
on their bed my siblings and I wrestle
    easy to consent to violence in the poem
when I spend the whole night knocking
    to the rhythm of a muffled scream
is still a scream as I sprout
                    into repetitions of the day
    kipling doesn't understand permanence
I trace the contours of a country I hesitate I claim
    control over the image as the digital
trace who languishes in English murmurs
    nothing is sacred in Tagalog
nothing exists unless felt
    as a tremor announced in the wake—

Rummaging through a bin of old photographs in the attic, I find a letter Lola wrote to me before I moved to Folsom from Manila with Mom and Dad.

                                Remember—

DRINK MILK OK?
Dear Princess Leia,
    Aimee Christine
    Sleeping Beauty, Cinderella
TAKE CARE of CASEY —
Remember?

    Then — we rode the
carab... , then the
waterfall, then the
dancing and singing.
    I miss you miss
you — love, —

translates to "Tandaan"

as I beg (in)   *Remember the time we rode the carabao*

with burden

Ayun! Sakupin na ang sagradong layunin

in indifference I

                    I miss you, miss you—

implode into slashes in my mouth

                                                      seized
                    Love, Lola

                                        Saan 'to galing?

saan 'to galing? Saan 'to galing?

    There are slashes

in my mouth   I don't know where they are from

Sakupin   ang banal na gantimpala—
                   I don't know where
                   I don't know where
Remember?

                   to find the form
                   (what) (do) I desire

"You didn't want me to hold you."
                   (ano) ng (ni) (na)nais ko

kipling, what do you do with language—

Sino ka ba?

who am I   to keep
who am I?

Sige, repeat.
Sige, repeat.
Sige, repeat.
Sige, repeat.
Sige, repeat.
Sige, repeat.

Yes, ulit-ulitin mo.

Ang wakas na hindi hinawakan

I would / rather / go through / tested / systems.

Kargahin mo ang dusa
Carry the burden.

At wag kang yumuko.
And don't bow down.

There is no other way to translate the poem.

THERE ARE SO MANY WAYS TO TRANSLATE THE POEM

NAPAKARAMING PAARAN MAGSALIN ANG TULA

THERE ARE TOO MANY WAYS TO TRANSLATE THE POEM

ANG DAMING PARAAN ISALIIN ANG (MGA) TEKSTO

THERE ARE SO MANY METHODS OF TRANSLATING TEXT

ANG DAMI-DAMING SISTEMA PARA MAUNAWAAN ANG SALITA

A MULTITUDE OF SYSTEMS TO UNDERSTAND SPEECH

LUBOS NG DAMI (NG?) SYSTEMS PARA INTINDIHAN ANG PAGSALITA

MASYADONG MARAMING SISTEMA TO COMPREHEND SPEAKING

A FLOOD OF PATHS PARA MAKOMPLETO ANG MGA SAL-ITA

BAHANG-BAHA ANG TEKSTO SA DAMI NG PARAAN NG MGA SINASABI

FLOODING-FLOOD THE TEXT IS SO MUCH WAYS OF SAY-INGS

BUMABAHA SA SOBRANG DAMI NA PARAANG KASABI-HAN

IT'S OVERPOURING WITH THE EXCESS OF PATHS NG KASABIHAN

UMAAGOS ANG SULAT SA DAMI NG PARAANG SUMABI

OVERFLOWING THE LETTER IT'S A LOT OF WAYS SPEAK-ING

UMAAPAW ANG LIHAM ANG DAMI-DAMI NG DAAN SUM-ALITA

INUNDATED THE LETTER WITH THE TONS OF WAYS THE ROAD SUMALITA

PUSPOS NA PUSPOS ANG LIHIN KASAMA ANG BIGAT NG PARAAN SUMASALITA ANG KALYE

THE LETTERS ARE SATURATED WITH THE HEAVINESS OF THE WAYS THE STREET SPEAKS

ANG LIHIM AY BINABABAD SA TIMBANG NG PAGSASAL-ITA NG DAAN

THE LETTER IS DRENCHED IN THE SCALE OF THE JOUR-
NEY'S SPEECH
YUNG LIHIM NA BASANG-BASA SA LOOB NG SUKAT NG
TALUMPATING LAKBAY
ANG/THE SULAT/WRITING NA/THAT UBODNGBASA/
SOFUCKINGWET/SA/LOCATED LAMAN/WITHIN NG/
BELONGINGTO SAKTO/FIT NG/POSSESSEDBY DISKUR-
SONG/SPEECHESTHAT DAANAN/TRAVEL
THEANG LETTERSUMUSULAT WHICHPARA THEHEIGH-
TOFREADING UTANGINAANGBASA WHEREDOONSA
MEATLOOB OFARINI EXACTSIKIP OWNEDKINUHANG
DISCOURSETHATKONBERSASYONNA PASSBYLAKBAY
THE/ANG/LET/TERSU/MU/SULA/TWH/ICH/PAR/AT/
HEHE/I/GH/TO/F/RE/A/DING/U/TAN/GIN/A/ANG/BAS/
AW/HER/EDO/ON/SAM/EAT/LO/OBOFARINIEX/ACTS/I/
KIP/OWNE/DKINUHANGD/ISCURSET/HATKO/NBER/SA/
SYON/NAPS/AS/B/YLAK/BA/Y/
YABKALAKYBSSAPANNOYSASREBONKTAHTESRUOC-
SIDGNAHUNIKDENWOPIKISTCAXEINIRAFOBOOLTAE-
MASNOODEREHWASABGNAANIGNATUGNIDAERFOTH-
GIEHEHTARAPHCIHWTALUSUMUSRETTELGNAEHT YA/
BKALA/KY/BSS/A/PAN/NOY/SASREB/ONK/T/AHTES/RU/
OCS/ID/GNAH/UNI/K/DEN/W/O/PIK/ISTCA/X/EIN/IR/
AFOBO/OL/TAEM/ASN/OODER/EHW/ASA/BGNAANI/
GNAT/UG/NID/AER/FOTH/GIEH/EH/TARA/PHCI/HWTAL/
US/UM/USR/ ETTEL/G /NA/EH/T YA BAKA AKALA KOY
BOSS NG PEN KNOW SAUCE RIBS HONK TI ATES RUE
OX EYED NGA YOU KNEE KAY DIN WE O' PEEK IT'S A
EEKS I'N ARE AFFABLE YULE TAME ASIAN ODOR WEW
ASA BAG NOW HONEY NOT UGH KNEED ERR FOUGHT
GUYERE HE TATARA POSSE HATOL HUSH AM USER
LITTLE GO NA EH NAEHT T NAEHT IT I NOT IT EYE
NOTE IT NOT ED KNOWTTED MATA KNOWEDED META
NODED MATANG ISANG PARAANG FORAWAYTOWARWAY-
TOWARDWAYWAITINGWAITINGSOMETHINGHUM-

MINGHUWHOWAITSWHOOMINTAYIMEANTIWHOHU-
MINTAYHUMINTAYWIKANGSAYSAYHUMINTAYWIKAN-
SAYSAYHUMINTAYWIKANGSAYSAYHUMINTAYWIKANG
SAYSAY SAYSAYHUMINTAYWIKANGSAYSAYHUMINTAY-
WIKANGSAYSAYSAYSAYHUMINTAYWIKANGSAYSAYHU-
MINTAYWIKANGSAYSAY HUMINTAYWIKANG SAYSAY
HUMINTAYWIKANG SAYSAYSAYSAYSAYSAYSAYSAYSAYSAY
SAYSAYSAYSAYSAYSAYSAYSAYSAYSAYSAYSAYSAYSAYSAY
SAYSAYSAYSAYSAYSAYSAYSAYSAYSAYSAYSAYSAYSAYSAY
SAYSAYSAYSAYSAYSAYSAYSAYSAYSAYSAYSAYSAYSAYSAY
SAYSAYSAYSAYSAYSAYSAYSAYSAYSAYSAYSAYSAYSAYSAY
SAYSAYSAYSAYSAYSAYSAYSAYSAYSAYSAYSAYSAYSAYSAY
SAYSAYSAYSAYSAYSAYSAYSAYSAYSAYSAYSAYSAYSAYSAY
SAYSAYSAYSAYSAYSAYSAYSAYSAYSAYSAYSAYSAYSAYSAY
SAYSAYSAYSAYSAYSAYSAYSAYSAYSAYSAYSAYSAYSAYSAY
SAYSAYSAYSAYSAYSAYSAYSAYSAYSAYSAYSAYSAYSAYSAY
SAYSAYSAYSAYSAYSAYSAYSAYSAYSAYSAYSAYSAYSAYSAY
SAYSAYSAYSAYSAYSAYSAYSAYSAYSAYSAYSAYSAYSAYSAY
SAYSAYSAYSAYSAYSAYSAYSAYSAYSAYSAYSAYSAYSAYSAY
SAYSAYSAYSAYSAYSAYSAYSAYSAYSAYSAYSAYSAYSAYSAY
SAYSAYSAYSAYSAYSAYSAYSAYSAYSAYSAYSAYSAYSAYSAY
SAYSAYSAYSAYSAYSAYSAYSAYSAYSAYSAYSAYSAYSAYSAY
SAYSAYSAYSAYSAYSAYSAYSAYSAYSAYSAYSAYSAYSAYSAY
SAYSAYSAYSAYSAYSAYSAYSAYSAYSAYSAYSAYSAYSAYSAY
SAYSAYSAYSAYSAYSAYSAYSAYSAYSAYSAYSAYSAYSAYSAY
SAYSAYSAYSAYSAYSAYSAYSAYSAYSAYSAYSAYSAYSAYSAY
SAYSAYSAYSAYSAYSAYSAYSAYSAYSAYSAYSAYSAYSAYSAY
SAYSAYSAYSAYSAYSAYSAYSAYSAYSAYSAYSAYSAYSAYSAY
SAYSAYSAYSAYSAYSAYSAYSAYSAYSAYSAYSAYSAYSAYSAY
SAYSAYSAYSAYSAYSAYSAYSAYSAYSAYSAYSAYSAYSAYSAY
SAYSAYSAYSAYSAYSAYSAYSAYSAYSAYSAYSAYSAYSAYSAY
SAYSAYSAYSAYSAYSAYSAYSAYSAYSAYSAYSAYSAYSAYSAY

I can almost taste

white canvas over brown bodies over brown bodies over brown bodies
over brown bodies over brown bodies over brown bodies over brown
bodies over brown bodies over brown bodies over brown bodies over
brown bodies over brown bodies over brown bodies over brown bodies
over brown bodies over brown bodies over brown bodies over brown
bodies over brown bodies over brown bodies over brown bodies over
brown bodies over brown bodies over brown bodies over brown bodies
over brown bodies over brown bodies over brown bodies over brown
bodies over brown bodies over brown bodies over brown bodies over
brown bodies over brown bodies over brown bodies over brown bod-
ies over brown bodies over brown bodies over brown bodies over
brown bodies over brown bodies over brown bodies over brown bod-
ies over brown bodies over brown bodies over brown bodies over
brown bodies over brown bodies over brown bodies over brown bodies

the wailing—

         —A less observed detail:
The corner, the dried-up puddle. I can almost hear the scratching of
metal—
   And if *Noli Me Tángere* is *The Spoliarium* incarnate—
    Sisa, Sisa, is that you?
Clasping tattered blue?
   Fallen from balete tree,
      no ache dull enough to stifle the screams
for the child who hears you sing
    his name on San Diego's streets—All I do is witness
     like the robed men rubbing their hands
like flies before a meal. Is it all technique?
   Luna, they say you are just
    like the masters.   The Ilustrado
      tames the beast— No, *Indio*

Bravo. Less renowned
   cowboy stance of a jaundice room
     and the foil pointed downward—
but the foil still held
   when the wrist cannot retreat—to unmask
    the brown is to concede
all claims to victory.   Dragged out
   of the amphitheater, do they bring the gladiators
    to Saturn for the soul to be devoured?
A less observed detail:
   the right corner inflected with a mound
    of rotting.
Plop another body and   the rest will slither
   like damp cloth in a pile of laundry.
    The archipelago is cracking

         Like you, Luna,
I have moved away.
   I return   in the summer to witness

a picture—the advertisement
of a drive-in motel hangs
from a line of police tape around the pieta
of a woman who holds her husband
on a blood-flood   street
in Manila—on a screen
as I was driven on what was
once the dictator's highway.   Lola returns
as a broken headlight on the freeway. Is it all technique?
The drying of a puddle. The chiaroscuro. The man
with his phone   captures their backs
in landscape mode as if to say
"Why be bound

to the frame?" 13.8 ft. × 25.18 ft. How literal,
upright by chains. Luna, must we render
the blind spots of our city?
The river of dead water, the dumping ground
where children play—I drown
out the wailing. But the salt
intrudes—Luna,
I am dragging—a deep inhale—   Sisa,
Sisa the centuries have not aged
you. We butcher   your grief until
all we have are entrails to feast   into monologue.

So hungry
for spectacle. The rising hands of a Roman master.
The president posed
with a clenched fist   as the bodies pile and the buildings
shield   the rotting. Saan natin dadamputin?
In the backyard   of my childhood home
a deceased dog is given a funeral.
And the earth swallows
wailing. Plop another body.

                                              Like you Luna,
        I can move away.
I get the headlines on a screen and mistake information
            for empathy—I hear they will build a new city.
                They will build a new city   inside
the same city. Who gets to look? I hear the river overflows
            but the dam is drained. I arch my back
                    after sleeping for too long. My sister laughs
and says, "Yoga pose." Repose. Yaya—don't say
            the maid—   still folds up   my play clothes.
                    I read about struggle
        while she cooks all my meals and there are days
where I forget   to say thank you.
                    There are days where
            I have learned to be less grateful.

        —Return,
            to the painting, return to the museum where
        replication is reality   and if replication is reality,
                    I am the audience   unsure
it should keep cheering.   In the silence, Sisa waddles
            through a car wreck and the orange flashing
                NO STOPPING   Speed up—all I do
                        is witness   like robed men
looking out from hotel windows
        to a city too busy   unveiling parking lot
                    white crosswalk—White out
            the shanties. White out the drought.
White out the gargling   of a road block body
                    from the press release. Where is the soul
        devoured? In the spaces a security camera swears
it doesn't record where my friends and I
            rolled splintered joints believing the clenched fist
                    was all technique and we didn't have to
throw out ballots we didn't sign up to read.

Our fathers said we could be anything
so we buried our bodies
        in reprieve   building forts
                out of newspapers until it rained so
hard the ink drip dripped   all over our skin
        is our skin   no matter how much dye—
Clot the puddle
        'til we can peel the scab. The muted cackle, the
                drying sampaguita leaves. Every shot
is a product of its lighting. Send me out as error. Exile to be
        exulted. The ex-pat laughs. The painting cannot
                breathe inside the flash
of crowds. The body is a scale. The gladiator is always
        dying. In our haste, another picture of—

                Sisa, Sisa could you take time to—
What do I ask? There is so much
                rotting. There is so much rotting.
        —Sisa, Sisa, saan ka dinampot? Rhyme
before reason. Rhyme is all revision. My roommate asks
        if poetry is the same thing as slogan.   Luna cackles
                in his grave. Yaya asks if I will remain in
America. Who gets to stay away? I pledge allegiance
        to the lyric. I pledge the lyric to the image. The
asphalt screams.   I'll always be afraid.
        I do not want to rest easy.
                        I let the paint speak.

It spits in my face

Where you call home
Saan ka babalik
Where you call home
Saan ka babalik
Where you call home
Saan ka babalik
Where you call home
Saan ka babalik
Where you call home
Saan ka babalik
Where you call home
Saan ka babalik
Where you call home
Saan ka babalik
Where you call home
Saan ka babalik
Where you call home
Saan ka babalik
Where you call home
Saan ka babalik
Where you call home
Saan ka babalik
Where you call home
Saan ka babalik
Where you call home
Saan ka babalik
Where you call home
Saan ka babalik
Where you call home
Saan ka babalik
Where you call home
Saan ka babalik

It knows I don't belong

so I return

to some semblance of beginning

where the tendrils promise not to petrify

into capillaries   where the eye is more than place-
            holder for prism   my father makes sure I am awake
before he gifts a book of words to learn
            in Tagalog   I am still
excited in the face of what swears is new
            proof of correspondence
                        the image of a person → tao
                        the image of a house → bahay
                        the image of a book → libro
                        the image of a child → bata
                        the image of a mother → nanay
                        the image of
a language is a landscape I discover
            not to pledge allegiance   to what hungers to be
earth rocking itself   back to sleep
            inside the urn Lola picks out
I try to become a weed that does not know
            it is sprouting   from the creases
of concrete that figures itself
            something so close   to home
hands erode as they press against the grain
            of eggshell wall   fissures from a flood
force us to move away   toward
            maybe   salvation can be found
on the diasporic OLED screen
            my siblings and I fill
the 4 × 4 fraction with our faces not touching
            not for a while   too far into the present
Wanting a beginning   to return to
            in the hour of reckoning
I assemble a cavalcade of stop signs
            puncturing   my eyes squint into California
sun I smudge   the windshield
            with palms deigning a stranger's grasp
during "Our Father" I get bored

I look through stained glass   as if it promises
to be something other than a prism   I lie flat
        into a plane insisting I get used to the turbulence
I run away 'til the GPS transmits my location
        into impression   I am trying
to articulate what I love about the word bulbundukin
        I am trying to discover how it simmered
into mountain range abscess occupied by suburb by new city by airport
by military by ex-pat by immigrant by—Where do you call— Ay nako!
Ito nanaman.

I've written the same poem again and again—I am so sorry
        this will never be a poem of contact
as it corrodes its own menagerie
        How does one predict a breakdown
without returning to a system
        of eulogies spread out against
"Have I told you about my first memory?"
        The mirror. The ex-pat jolted
                into the bedroom of an apartment in Folsom,
California where my father and I march on the arms
        of our living room couches
to "Do You Hear the People Sing?" like it matters
        say it to be met with disbelief—
                        "Did you choose your last name?"

My father and I are Imperial
        as he reads me a bedtime story   about a father
constructing a ladder to fetch his daughter a fracture
        of the moon   turning away
from light—   The first time I encounter "Imperial"
        I see it plastered outside a furniture store
with chairs lacquered in gold when I am too young
        to know how to look things up
I keep them to myself   and make meaning from sound

                    mistake sanggol → flower
                            kalsada → horse
                            leeg → leg
                            higit → less
                            lipat → fly
it is true until I find out it isn't
            pulsations of a finish line
by line the poem aspires to be music
            while afraid of time—I am a child again and I leave
my fingers on Lola's lips as she sings me back to sleep
            "Que sera, sera"   say it to be met with disbelief
when it's all in service of art   stay away from me
                            tendrils mistake every wall as
antique mouth disfigures into speaker dispersing
            instructions toward language projected as empathy
then decide   "How fragile do you want to be"
            who gets to write a poem of technique
why write the poem of technique
            the text to speech machine's sibilance
so easy to crave   in this heat
            branches shatter away   the poem aspires waste

remote from control too literal to be frightening
            cheers of a metal detector
doing its job   sharp turn   my mother
            with me at baggage claim I don't want to admit
I'll miss her as her exhales conduct the overture
            to weeping I flood the silence with motif:

sige repeat sige repeat sige repeat sige repeat sige repeat sige repeat sige
repeat sige repeat sige repeat sige repeat sige repeat sige repeat sige repeat
sige repeat sige repeat sige repeat sige repeat sige repeat sige repeat

Sige—I'm doing it wrong
            not being able to distinguish between resistance

and curation of longing   for something other
     than local shades of brown bodies over brown
bodies over brown bodies over brown bodies over brown bodies over
brown bodies over brown bodies over brown over brown over brown
womb destined to rupture
the return to some sort of beginning na hindi ko kayang
intindihan   ang pagnanasa
               sa simula sa simula sa simula sa simula sa simula sa simula sa
simula sa simula na
          ang gulo   ang gulo ang gulo ang gulo ang gulo
ang gulo   "Ang gulo-gulo ng kwarto mo, Christine!
                              Hindi ka ang daigdig!"
I have so much to explain
          I let the room fester   'til it forces out
particulates of my gritting skin   blessed with proof
     of baptism   I wash my hands in holy water
since it's free someone
          pigilin mo siya pigilin mo siya pigilin mo siya pigilin mo siya
pigilin mo siya pigilin mo siya pigilin—
stop my muscles from stuttering
          nakakahiya ang language is embarrassing
"How certain are you   this is all speculative"
     I want to be something other than sorry
I want to belong   as mistake
     carves itself into synapse sighing
nothing here can be fossilized
     into memorial   I am ready
the sash across my back reads disgrace
          in every language I speak may tinatago ako
at   walang dadating sa sulok walang may alam
ang dusa   ko as if I, too, were not
the rattling of a cage the ex-pat walks away from
          proclaims   "We will never be the same"
I'm getting somewhere

and my hands rise with the Roman master as we breathe the arid air of
you over you over you over you over you over you over you over you
over you over you over you over you over you over you over you over
you over you over you over you over you over you over you over you
over you over you over you over you over you over you over you over
you over you over you over you over you over you over you over you
over you over you over you over you over you over you over you over
you over you over you over you over you over you over you over you
over you over you over you over you over you over you over you over
you over you over you over you over you over you over you over you
over you over you over you over you over you over you over you over
you over you over you over you over you over you over you over you
over you over you over you over you over you over you over you over
you over you over you over you over you over you over you over you
over you over you over you over you over you over you over you over
you over you over you over you over you over you over you over you
over you over you over you over you over you over you over you over
you over you over you over you over you over you over you over you
over you over you over you over you over you over you over you over
you over you over you over you over you over you over you over you
over you over you over you over you over you over you over you over
you over you over you over you over you over you over you over you
over you over you over you over you over you over you over you over
you over you over you over you over you over you over you over you
over you over you over you over you over you over you over you over
you over you over you over you over you over you over you over you
over you over you over you over you over you over you over you over
you over you over you over you over you over you over you over you
over you over you over you over you over you over you over you over
you over you over you over you over you over you over you over you
over you over you over you over you over you over you over you over
you over you over you over you over you over you over you over you
over you over you over you over you over you over you over you over you

over you over you over you over you over you over you over you over
you over you over you over you over you over you over you over you
over you over you over you over you over you over you over you over
you over you over you over you over you over you over you over you
over you over you over you over you over you over you over you over
you over you over you over you over you over you over you over you
over you over you over you over you over you over you over you over
you over you over you over you over you over you over you over you
over you over you over you over you over you over you over you over
you over you over you over you over you over you over you over you
over you over you over you over you over you over you over you over
you over you over you over you over you over you over you over you
over you over you over you over you over you over you over you over
you over you over you over you over you over you over you over you
over you over you over you over you over you over you over you over
you over you over you over you over you over you over you over you
over you over you over you over you over you over you over you over
you over you over you over you over you over you over you over you
over you over you over you over you over you over you over you over
you over you over you over you over you over you over you over you
over you over you over you over you over you over you over you over
you over you over you over you over you over you over you over you
over you over you over you over you over you over you over you over
you over you over you over you over you over you over you over you
over you over you over you over you over you over you over you over
you over you over you over you over you over you over you over you
over you over you over you over you over you over you over you over
you over you over you over you over you over you over you over you
over you over you over you over you over you over you over you over
you over you over you over you over you over you over you over you
over you over you over you over you over you over you over you over you

laugh with me as the photograph reads   *Remember*

where delight emerges through the echo of our dissonance where I will
one day receive the earth floating above where I live where I am left to
carry this weight where only memory can comfort manatili ka manatili
ka muna para makita mo ang bumubunga sa kaguluhan ng dila where
I no longer mistake sikip for held slowly into the light why bring you
here para matandaan mo ang talim ng gunita ang tamis ng biso there is
so much rotting sa dumi ng salamin nakilalang-kilala mo yung

please let me splinter please gusto kong manatili gusto kong lumayas
gusto kong manatili gustong-gusto ko gusto kong—I am still translating,   Ako—

Kinakarga ko ang dusa

At what cost does the mirror remain
Anong iniiwan ko para sa salamin
At what cost does the mirror remain
Anong iniiwan ko para sa salamin
At what cost does the mirror remain
Anong iniiwan ko para sa salamin
At what cost does the mirror remain
Anong iniiwan ko para sa salamin
At what cost does the mirror remain
Anong iniiwan ko para sa salamin
At what cost does the mirror remain
Anong iniiwan ko para sa salamin
At what cost does the mirror remain
Anong iniiwan ko para sa salamin
At what cost does the mirror remain
Anong iniiwan ko para sa salamin

Carrying I, the burden

Notes

The amateur quality of certain translations of Kipling's poem is intentional, since I tried my best to write the translation myself rather than have someone guide me throughout as a way to practice my Tagalog and contend with what I know and don't know. Aside from help from my grandmother and online dictionaries, I wrote all of the Tagalog, which may not be entirely perfect. I am always going to be a student of the language.

Certain names have been changed to protect the identity of the persons.

Autobiographical notes on Kipling are primarily taken from Patrick Brantlinger's "Kipling's 'The White Man's Burden' and Its Afterlives" and *The Long Recessional: The Imperial Life of Rudyard Kipling,* by David Gilmour, among other sources, mainly internet research.

"A Common Characteristic of Tagalog is the Repetition of a Word" should not be taken as representative of the rules of any type of linguistics.

The line "Each time life breaks the circle, the games turn gray and ridiculous" is from Ingmar Bergman's *Through a Glass Darkly.*

The text on pages 207 and 210 is composed/collaged of text from the pages of websites of multiple Philippine Consulates in the US on Dual Citizenship along with text from the webpages of the UCIS on US and

Dual Citizenship, the Philippine's Bureau of Immigration on Dual Citizenship, the IRS webpage on US citizens who acquire income abroad, and the mentioned websites' webpages on renunciation of citizenship.

Sisa is the mother who dies while searching for her missing sons in Jose Rizal's novel *Noli Me Tángere*. Her soliloquys are the equivalent of Hamlet's "To be, or not to be." A quick search on YouTube will provide you with a number of performances of Sisa's grief.

Indio Bravo is a self-portrait by Juan Luna.

Acknowledgments

To everyone who has read this book, I am so grateful to you. Salamat.

I am grateful to the following publications and their respective editors for publishing sections of *Mistaken for an Empire*:

REFILL: An Anthology in Decolonial Ekphrasis
Poetry
Inverted Syntax
TLDTD
Slipping Through: CalArts MFA Writing 2020 Anthology
Under the Belly of the Beast
New Poetry, California Poets
Lunch Ticket
Rambutan Literary
No Tokens

I am extremely grateful to everyone at Mad Creek Books and The Ohio State University Press for all the effort and time they put into bringing *Mistaken for an Empire* into the world. To my editor, Kristen Elias Rowley, I am so thankful for your guidance, patience, and belief in my work.

I am grateful to CalArts, and specifically the students and faculty in the MFA in Creative Writing Program. I thank my cohort and my friends from CalArts who helped me understand the importance of community in creativity and criticality. I am especially so thankful for Matthew Bussa and Sarah Yanni, two incredible poets who are also 2/3 of our supreme platonic throuple. My manuscript would not be what it is without the guidance and mentorship of the following faculty: Michael Leong, Gabrielle Civil, and Victoria Chang. I am deeply indebted to Jon Wagner, my mentor both in and outside of academia. Jon, your unwavering dedication to both this book and my growth as a writer and scholar has been crucial in getting me to where I am today.

I am grateful to the BFA in Creative Writing Program at Ateneo de Manila University, where I first learned how to be a better writer and scholar, and to all the people from there who continue to be such beams of light in my life. Shout out to Nikay Paredes, Ayana Tolentino, Cathy Dario, and Tiffany Conde.

I thank all of my friends, with special thanks to my closest friends, Julian Occena, Kael Noriega, Marti Salud, Danica Alagon, Mia Parma, Sienna Nacario, Lessan Aristoza, Robs Tenefrancia, Marga Olivares, Dewi Manuel, Nissy Suarez, Rosa Evangelina, and Mantis Lux for being there for and with me.

I am always grateful to my family. The Cornels, especially Mom and Mama Rose, for your love and support. The Cabals for always cheering me on. Big shout out to Uncle Benjo for providing a place to go when I'm homesick and being the reason I will always return to LA. The Imperials, for seeing me through it all and continuing to do so even when we're thousands of miles away from each other. My cousins Chris, Joey, Tommy, and Vinny, for reminding me what it means to play. Ninang, for teaching me what it means to know and to love art. Mama Cathy, for hugging me tight and reminding me there's always a reason to be happy. Lolo, for being the encyclopedia of knowledge I will always aspire to be. And my siblings, Casey, JP, and Camille, for being the best wolf pack anyone could ask for—I love you guys so much.

I cannot thank Simone Zapata, my beautiful partner in everything, enough. Thank you for holding me. Thank you for the life we continue to build together.

This book is dedicated to Dad and Lola, the two people in my life who have shown me what unconditional love and pride are. No amount of thanks will ever suffice.

Dad, I carry you in everything I do. I am so proud to be your daughter. I love you.

Lola, mahal na mahal kita. Ikaw ang una kong guro, kaibigan, at idolo. Ikaw ang rason na natatagumpay ako.

21st CENTURY ESSAYS

David Lazar and Patrick Madden, Series Editors

This series from Mad Creek Books is a vehicle to discover, publish, and promote some of the most daring, ingenious, and artistic nonfiction. This is the first and only major series that announces its focus on the essay—a genre whose plasticity, timelessness, popularity, and centrality to nonfiction writing make it especially important in the field of nonfiction literature. In addition to publishing the most interesting and innovative books of essays by American writers, the series publishes extraordinary international essayists and reprint works by neglected or forgotten essayists, voices that deserve to be heard, revived, and reprised. The series is a major addition to the possibilities of contemporary literary nonfiction, focusing on that central, frequently chimerical, and invariably supple form: The Essay.

Mistaken for an Empire: A Memoir in Tongues *
Christine Imperial

Everything I Never Wanted to Know
Christine Hume

Engine Running: Essays
Cade Mason

Ripe: Essays
Negesti Kaudo

Dark Tourist: Essays *
Hasanthika Sirisena

Supremely Tiny Acts: A Memoir of a Day
Sonya Huber

Art for the Ladylike: An Autobiography through Other Lives
Whitney Otto

The Terrible Unlikelihood of Our Being Here
Susanne Paola Antonetta

Warhol's Mother's Pantry: Art, America, and the Mom in Pop *
M. I. Devine

How to Make a Slave and Other Essays
Jerald Walker

Don't Look Now: Things We Wish We Hadn't Seen
Edited by Kristen Iversen and David Lazar

Just an Ordinary Woman Breathing
Julie Marie Wade

*Annual Gournay Prize Winner